MASTERING FOREX

The Essential Guide to Trading Success and Smart Risk Management

Nathan Venture, D.

Contents

Introduction

Before any chart, indicator, or trade idea earns your attention, one principle needs to be clear: the foreign exchange market is not a machine that hands out predictable outcomes. It is a constantly shifting network of participants, information, and order flow. Price moves because large and small players are adjusting exposure, reacting to news, hedging business needs, or speculating on future conditions. That reality matters because it explains why the same setup can work well one week and struggle the next. The job of the trader is not to force certainty onto the market, but to build a process that can respond to uncertainty with discipline.

Forex is also different from many other markets in the way it is structured. It is decentralized, global, and active around the clock during the trading week. There is no single exchange that sets a universal price. Instead, prices are formed across a network of banks, electronic communication platforms, brokers, institutions, corporations, and retail traders. This structure creates deep liquidity in the major pairs, but it also means that conditions can change quickly when trading flows concentrate in one session or when a major economic release hits the wires. Understanding that environment is essential because it shapes everything from spread behavior to volatility to execution quality [8].

For the trader, the first practical lesson is that not all currency pairs behave the same way. Major pairs tend to offer the most liquidity and the tightest spreads, which often makes them more suitable for new traders who need cleaner execution and more stable trading conditions. Minor pairs and exotic pairs can offer larger moves, but they usually come with wider spreads, thinner liquidity, and more erratic price behavior. That does not make them untradeable; it simply means they demand more caution, more selective timing, and a stronger understanding of the forces behind the move. A pair that looks attractive because of its volatility can be costly if the spread, slippage, or news risk overwhelms the edge.

Liquidity is one of the most important concepts in forex, but it is often misunderstood. High liquidity does not mean price is always calm. It means there is a large pool of buyers and sellers, which generally helps keep transaction costs lower and execution smoother. In the most active pairs, price can still move sharply when large orders hit the market or when sentiment shifts quickly. In thinner pairs, the same size order can create a much larger price impact. This is why traders must think beyond direction and consider the quality of the market they are trading. A setup that appears identical on two different pairs may carry very different risk because of the underlying liquidity profile.

Market participants also shape how forex behaves. Commercial companies may be hedging international cash flows. Asset managers may be adjusting currency exposure tied to global portfolios. Banks and large institutions may be managing inventory, facilitating client orders, or positioning around macro expectations. Central banks can intervene directly or indirectly when they believe exchange rate moves threaten policy goals, and research has shown that intervention can be effective in smoothing exchange-rate paths under some conditions [4]. Retail traders are a smaller part of the overall market, but they still contribute to short-term flow, especially around technical levels and well-followed news events. The important point is that no single participant group controls the market all the time; price is the result of many motives colliding.

Because forex is tied so closely to the global economy, trading sessions matter. Activity tends to rise and fall with the opening and closing of major financial centers, and volatility often expands when London and New York overlap. Some pairs are most active during specific regional sessions because their underlying economies and participants are concentrated in those hours. A trader who ignores session timing may misread a quiet market as weak interest or mistake a temporary burst of activity for a lasting trend. Session awareness helps you avoid forcing trades when conditions are thin and helps you focus when the market is most likely to deliver movement.

Volatility is not just a measure of how much price moves; it is a measure of how much uncertainty the market is pricing in. Sometimes volatility comes from scheduled events such as inflation data, employment reports, central bank decisions, or policy speeches. Sometimes it comes from unscheduled shocks, geopolitical developments, or sudden changes in risk sentiment. Exchange rates are especially sensitive because they reflect expectations about interest rates, growth, inflation, and capital flows. A currency can strengthen on better economic data, but it can also weaken if the market had already priced in even stronger results. The reaction matters as much as the number itself.

This is where many developing traders get tripped up: they focus on finding a direction instead of understanding the conditions that support a trade. A strong trend, a range, a breakout, and a reversal do not all require the same market environment. A trend-following approach usually works best when one side of the market has a clear advantage and price is moving with momentum. Range strategies require a market that is balanced and mean-reverting. Breakout strategies need enough compression and participation to sustain expansion. If you mismatch strategy and environment, even a well-designed method can produce disappointing results.

Another key lesson is that forex prices are influenced by expectations, not just outcomes. If traders expect a central bank to raise rates, the currency may rise before the announcement. If the decision matches expectations but the accompanying statement sounds cautious, the currency can still fall. This is why "buy the rumor, sell the news" is such a common pattern in currency trading. The market often moves ahead of the event, then reassesses once the event is public. Traders who understand this dynamic are less likely to chase headlines and more likely to think in terms of positioning, surprise, and revision.

Because the market is decentralized, there is no single tape that reveals the whole story. You see price, spreads, and perhaps volume proxies from your platform, but you do not see the full order flow of the global market. That means forex traders must work with incomplete information and avoid pretending otherwise. Strong trading does not come from knowing everything; it comes from knowing enough to make a controlled decision. You assess the pair, the session, the event calendar, the broader trend, and the risk on the table, then you decide whether the opportunity is worth taking.

Technology has also changed the market's behavior. Electronic trading has increased speed, broadened access, and made price discovery more efficient. At the same time, it has made the market more competitive and more sensitive to algorithmic participation. Many short-term moves are now influenced by automated systems reacting to price, volatility, and news in fractions of a second. Research across financial prediction has also shown that machine learning methods can improve forecasting performance in some contexts, although they do not eliminate uncertainty or guarantee trading success [2]. For the retail trader, the lesson is not to imitate institutional technology, but to respect how quickly the market can adapt.

That is why a professional mindset begins with realism. The forex market offers opportunity, but it also punishes carelessness, overconfidence, and poor risk control. It rewards traders who can observe structure, adapt to changing conditions, and preserve capital when the environment is unfavorable. If you treat the market as a place to predict every move, you will likely overtrade. If you treat it as a place to identify edges, manage exposure, and wait for favorable conditions, you give yourself a much better chance of lasting long enough to improve.

In practice, that means learning to ask a different set of questions before every trade:

- Which participants are likely driving this move?
- Is the market liquid enough for clean execution?
- What session am I trading, and is volatility likely to expand or contract?
- Is the pair behaving like a trend, a range, or a transition?
- What event or expectation could change the current price behavior?

Those questions do not replace a strategy. They make a strategy usable. A trading system without market context is fragile. A trading plan built on awareness of market structure, liquidity, and volatility is far more resilient. The rest of the book builds on that foundation by showing how to read the market, manage risk, and execute with consistency.

CHAPTER 1

Chapter 1: Understanding the Forex Market Landscape

The foreign exchange market is best understood as a living network rather than a single exchange or centralized venue, and that distinction matters because it shapes how price forms, how orders interact, and how opportunities appear across the day. Before moving into specific pairs, participants, and session behavior, it helps to establish the basic structure of the market environment traders are stepping into: one that is decentralized, deeply interconnected, and constantly influenced by global business activity, policy expectations, and shifting demand for currencies. Electronic trading has expanded that reach and changed how market access and price discovery work [15], which is one reason forex remains so dynamic and so widely traded.

How the foreign exchange market operates and why it is the world's largest financial market

The foreign exchange market operates as a decentralized network of banks, brokers, electronic communication platforms, corporations, hedge funds, asset managers, and individual traders, all interacting across time zones rather than through a single central exchange. That structure is one reason it remains so active: there is no closing bell for the market as a whole, only a continuous handoff from one major financial center to the next. As trading moves from Sydney to Tokyo, then to London and New

York, prices are constantly being updated by new orders, changing expectations, and shifting liquidity conditions. In practical terms, this means forex is not a market where one participant sets the price; it is a market where price emerges from competition between buyers and sellers at every moment.

Because currencies are quoted in pairs, every transaction involves simultaneous exposure to two economies and two sets of expectations. When a trader buys EUR/USD, for example, the trade is not simply a bet on the euro rising in isolation; it is a judgment that the euro will strengthen relative to the U.S. dollar. That relative-value structure is central to how the market functions. Exchange rates reflect differences in interest rates, inflation, growth prospects, trade flows, and risk sentiment, and they also influence those same forces by affecting import costs, export competitiveness, and capital movement [8]. This feedback loop gives forex its depth and complexity: currencies are both instruments of exchange and indicators of broader economic conditions.

The market's size comes from the sheer scale of global currency use. Every international trade settlement, cross-border investment, overseas payroll, tourist exchange, and corporate hedge creates demand for one currency and supply of another. Multinational firms convert revenues, pension funds rebalance international holdings, and banks facilitate client transactions on a massive scale. Unlike many other markets, forex is not driven only by speculative activity; it is also supported by constant real-world need. That underlying utility creates a continuous stream of transactions, which is why the market's daily turnover exceeds that of equities and most fixed-income markets by a wide margin. In other words, forex is large not just because traders like to speculate on it, but because the global economy depends on it.

Liquidity is another reason the market is dominant. Major currency pairs can absorb substantial order flow with relatively tight spreads because so many participants are active at once. Large banks and electronic trading systems provide continuous pricing, while institutional clients and retail traders add additional flow. Over time, the market has become increasingly electronic, with much of the price discovery process shifting away from voice dealing and toward automated matching and platform-based execution [21]. That evolution has made the market faster, more accessible, and more transparent in some respects, while also increasing the importance of execution quality, latency, and spread awareness for traders who enter and exit frequently.

The decentralized structure also explains why forex can feel efficient and unpredictable at the same time. Efficient, because information is absorbed quickly when major economic data, central bank statements, or geopolitical events hit the market. Unpredictable, because no single exchange controls the order book, and liquidity can change abruptly depending on time of day, news intensity, and the risk appetite of larger participants. A trader may see calm conditions in one session and sharp movement in another simply because the underlying flow of orders has changed. This is one reason the market rewards preparation: the same pair can trade smoothly during active overlap hours and become thin and erratic when major centers are quiet.

For traders, the important takeaway is that forex pricing is not random noise; it is the visible outcome of a global allocation process. Companies hedge business exposure, governments and institutions move capital, and speculators position for changes in policy, growth, and sentiment. Because exchange rates influence inflation, output, and international capital flows, they sit at the intersection of macroeconomics and market behavior [8]. That is what makes the market so large and so tradable. It is not merely a place where prices move; it is a system through which the world continuously revalues money itself.

Major currency pairs, minor pairs, and exotic pairs: what traders need to know

Currency pairs are not all traded with the same conditions, and that difference matters as much as the direction of price itself. The market groups pairs into three broad categories: major pairs, minor pairs, and exotic pairs. Each category has its own liquidity profile, spread behavior, and sensitivity to news, and those traits influence how easily a trader can enter, manage, and exit a position. A pair that looks attractive on a chart can still be a poor trading vehicle if it is expensive to trade or prone to erratic gaps and slippage.

Major pairs are the most widely traded combinations in forex and almost always include the U.S. dollar. Examples include EUR/USD, USD/JPY, GBP/USD, USD/CHF, AUD/USD, USD/CAD, and NZD/USD. These pairs typically offer the tightest spreads and the deepest liquidity because they are heavily used by banks, institutions, multinational businesses, and speculators. That depth tends to make them more suitable for most retail traders, especially those who are still learning execution discipline. When liquidity is strong, orders are generally filled more efficiently, price movement is often smoother, and transaction costs are easier to control. The broad participation in these pairs also reflects the central role of major currencies in trade, investment, and reserve management [8].

Minor pairs, sometimes called cross-currency pairs, do not include the U.S. dollar. Common examples are EUR/GBP, EUR/JPY, GBP/JPY, AUD/NZD, and EUR/AUD. These pairs can still be highly liquid, especially when they involve other major currencies, but they often behave differently from the dollar pairs many traders first study. Because their price action reflects the relationship between two non-dollar economies, they may respond more directly to regional policy shifts, relative growth expectations, and sentiment differences between the two currencies involved. That can create opportunities, but it also requires a trader to understand more than one economic backdrop at the same time. A move in EUR/GBP, for instance, may tell a different story than a move in EUR/USD even if the euro is the common denominator.

Exotic pairs combine a major currency with a currency from a smaller or emerging economy, such as USD/TRY, USD/MXN, EUR/SEK, or GBP/ZAR. These pairs tend to have wider spreads, lower liquidity, and larger price jumps than majors or many minors. They can also be more vulnerable to sudden repricing when local political events, capital controls, inflation surprises, or central bank actions change expectations quickly. For that reason, exotic pairs often demand more caution with position sizing and stop placement. A stop that would be reasonable in a major pair may be too tight in an exotic pair, where normal volatility can be much more aggressive. Traders who choose these instruments should do so deliberately, not because the chart appears active, but because they understand the risks that come with thinner trading conditions.

Spread and liquidity differences are not just technical details; they affect the quality of every decision. A pair with a one-pip spread and deep order flow gives the trader more room to work than a pair with a wide spread that immediately places the trade at a disadvantage. This matters most for short-term traders, scalpers, and anyone who enters and exits frequently. A strategy that appears profitable on chart data can lose its edge once spreads, slippage, and execution delays are included. In less liquid pairs, the visible price may move smoothly while the actual tradable price jumps around the quote. That makes risk control more difficult, especially during news releases or periods when market participation is thin.

Volatility also varies by pair, and traders should expect that variation rather than treat it as random noise. JPY pairs often become more active during Asian trading hours and around shifts in global risk sentiment. Commodity-linked currencies such as the Australian dollar, New Zealand dollar, and Canadian dollar may be influenced by resource prices and trade expectations. European pairs can become especially responsive during the London session, when market depth increases and major economic releases hit the tape. These patterns do not guarantee direction, but they help explain why some pairs are better suited to certain strategies and trading windows than others.

Another useful way to think about pair selection is in terms of what drives the move. In major pairs, the U.S. dollar often acts as the benchmark, so traders may need to focus on both the dollar side and the countercurrency side of the pair. In minor pairs, relative strength between two non-dollar economies becomes more important. In exotic pairs, local conditions can dominate in ways that are less visible on mainstream financial calendars. Exchange rates are shaped by trade flows, capital flows, inflation, and broader macroeconomic conditions [8], so the pair you choose should match the kind of information you are prepared to follow. A trader who prefers clean technical setups may find majors more manageable, while a trader with strong macro awareness may see opportunities in minors or exotics that others avoid.

It is also worth noting that market structure continues to evolve. Electronic trading, changing liquidity provision, and the growing influence of algorithmic execution have altered how pairs trade at different times of day and under different conditions [8]. At the same time, newer forms of digital money and payment experimentation may influence future currency usage and cross-border flows [28]. For the forex trader, the practical lesson is straightforward: pair behavior is not fixed. A currency pair is a product of both its underlying economics and the market environment in which it trades. Choosing the right pair means choosing the right combination of liquidity, volatility, cost, and information burden for your strategy and account size.

Market participants, liquidity, and the role of banks, institutions, and retail traders

The foreign exchange market is often described as decentralized, but for a trader it is more useful to think of it as an ecosystem of different participants competing and cooperating through price. Banks, nonbank financial institutions, corporations, hedge funds, asset managers, brokers, and retail traders all interact in the same market, yet they do not participate for the same reasons. Some are trying to reduce business risk, some are reallocating capital, and some are seeking short-term profit from price movement. Those different motives matter because they create the order flow that drives liquidity, volatility, and the quality of the prices available at any given moment. Research on FX market structure shows that the market has evolved into a highly electronic and interconnected network, with trading increasingly organized around platforms and algorithmic execution rather than old-style voice dealing [8][15][18].

At the center of this system are the large banks and other major liquidity providers. These firms stand between buyers and sellers, continuously quoting prices and facilitating transactions for clients and for their own books. In practical terms, they are one of the main reasons major currency pairs can be traded with tight spreads and deep order books. Their role is not simply to "move price" in a direct sense, but to absorb, distribute, and repackage flow from many sources. A corporate payment order, a hedge fund position change, and a central bank-related reaction can all pass through the same liquidity channels, and the resulting price adjustment reflects the balance of that flow. Because of their size and network access, banks often see the broadest picture of market activity, but they are also constrained by inventory risk, capital requirements, and the need to manage exposure carefully.

Institutions such as hedge funds, pension managers, mutual funds, sovereign entities, and corporates contribute a different kind of flow. Corporations are often in the market to hedge future receipts or payments, not to speculate on direction. Asset managers may be adjusting currency exposure tied to international portfolios. Hedge funds and proprietary trading firms are more likely to seek return from relative value, macro themes, momentum, or short-term inefficiencies. These participants can create strong directional pressure when many of them respond to the same macro catalyst or technical level. Their orders are often larger and more deliberate than retail orders, and they may be executed over time to reduce market impact. That means the effect of institutional activity is not always immediate on the chart, but it can shape the broader trend and the behavior around key levels.

Liquidity is the practical outcome of all this interaction. When liquidity is abundant, traders can enter and exit with less slippage, narrower spreads, and more predictable fills. When liquidity thins, the market becomes more sensitive to even modest order flow, and price can move quickly through levels that might otherwise hold. This is why the same pair can feel calm during one session and erratic during another. Liquidity is not constant; it expands and contracts with the trading day, the news calendar, and the willingness of participants to commit capital. Electronic trading has made this more visible and more immediate, because prices now adjust continuously across venues and time zones rather than through a slower dealer-driven process [15]. For the retail trader, the key point is that a chart pattern does not exist in isolation from market depth. A clean setup is more reliable when liquidity is supportive and less reliable when the market is thin or event risk is high.

Retail traders are the smallest participants individually, but together they form a meaningful part of the market's activity. Their influence is usually indirect rather than dominant. Retail order flow tends to be more fragmented, more sentiment-driven, and more sensitive to leverage and emotion. That does not make retail traders irrelevant; it means their edge must come from discipline, not size. Because retail traders typically access the market through brokers and platforms that aggregate liquidity from larger providers, the prices they see are the result of a layered system rather than a direct one-to-one exchange. This structure can be an advantage because it opens the market to small accounts, but it also means retail traders are often reacting to a market shaped by participants with better information flow, lower transaction costs, and more sophisticated execution tools.

Algorithmic and high-speed trading have added another layer to this environment. A growing share of modern FX activity is routed through systems that can analyze, quote, hedge, and execute far faster than a discretionary trader can respond [31][32][18]. These systems do not make the market random, but they do make it more efficient at incorporating information and more competitive around short-term opportunities. For the retail trader, that has two implications. First, very short-lived inefficiencies are harder to capture consistently. Second, execution quality matters more than ever, because a good idea can be weakened by poor fills, excessive spread, or chasing price after the move has already occurred. In a market where large participants may react in milliseconds, the retail trader has to be selective about time frame, timing, and the type of setup being traded.

Understanding who is active in the market also helps explain why price reacts differently to different kinds of information. A central bank comment may trigger one response from banks managing inventory, another from macro funds adjusting exposure, and a third from retail traders following momentum. The resulting move is not just a headline reaction; it is the combined effect of multiple participant groups reassessing risk at the same time. That is why it is often more useful to ask, "Who needs to buy or sell here?" than simply "What is the news?" The answer points you toward the likely source of liquidity, the strength of the move, and the probability that price will continue or stall once the initial reaction has passed.

Trading sessions, volatility patterns, and the impact of global economic activity

Trading sessions matter because the forex market does not move with the same intensity at all hours. Price can drift quietly during one session and then expand sharply when a major financial center comes online. The key sessions—Sydney, Tokyo, London, and New York—create a repeating rhythm in liquidity and volatility. That rhythm is not random. It reflects when banks are active, when regional economic data is released, and when large institutional orders are most likely to enter the market. A trader who understands this rhythm gains a practical advantage: the chart is no longer just a line of candles, but a record of changing participation.

Liquidity tends to be highest when sessions overlap, especially during the London-New York overlap. In those hours, spreads often tighten and price can move more efficiently because more participants are competing to transact. That does not mean every overlap produces a clean trend, but it does mean the market is usually better suited to active trading than the quieter hours between major centers. By contrast, the Asian session often produces more restrained movement in many major pairs, though pairs tied to the yen, Australian dollar, or New Zealand dollar may be more active. This is why the same strategy can perform differently depending on the time of day. A breakout method that works well during London may struggle when volume is thin and price is more likely to stall.

Volatility is also shaped by the type of session rather than just its size. The London open often brings a burst of repositioning as European traders respond to overnight developments and prepare for the day's data releases. New York can add another layer of volatility, especially when U.S. economic reports or central bank commentary are on deck. These bursts are important because they often create the sharpest intraday opportunities, but they also carry a greater risk of slippage and false starts. A candle that looks decisive in a low-activity period may be far less meaningful than the same candle printed during a session open or major news release. Electronic trading has made this flow more continuous and more global, but it has not removed the session-based character of participation [15].

Global economic activity shapes these patterns by determining when traders are most motivated to act. Scheduled data releases such as inflation, employment, GDP, and rate decisions can transform a relatively calm session into a high-volatility environment within seconds. Beyond the calendar, broader economic conditions matter too. When markets are focused on growth differentials, inflation surprises, or central bank policy divergence, currency pairs can trend more persistently because capital is being repriced across regions. Research on price discovery in the foreign exchange market shows that exchange rates respond to information in a distributed way rather than through a single source, which helps explain why different sessions can contribute differently to the formation of price [37]. In practical terms, this means a trader should not treat all movement as equal; the context behind the move matters as much as the move itself.

There is also an important relationship between intraday volatility and the appearance of sudden jumps. Forex prices can move in smooth sequences for long stretches and then reprice abruptly when new information enters the market. These jumps are especially relevant around session opens, surprise data, and periods when liquidity is uneven. A recent review of intraday financial data emphasizes that jumps are a central feature of market dynamics and a key concern for risk management [39]. For the trader, that means stop placement, position size, and trade timing should reflect the possibility of discontinuous movement, not just average candle size. A market that looks orderly on a five-minute chart can still gap several pips in an instant when a news catalyst hits.

The practical implication is that session awareness should become part of trade selection, not just trade management. If a setup appears during a quiet period, it may need confirmation from the next active session before it deserves commitment. If a pair is already extended into a major overlap, chasing the first spike may expose the trader to a late entry and poor reward potential. The best opportunities often appear when session behavior aligns with the broader economic story: a pair tied to a strong trend may continue moving during the session where its most relevant participants are active, while a range-bound pair may be better suited to slower conditions and tighter targets. Electronic trading has made it easier for participants across time zones to respond quickly, but it has also made the market more sensitive to concentrated bursts of order flow [14][15].

This is why a trader should study not only the direction of price, but also the clock behind it. A chart viewed at 2 a.m. local market time may tell a very different story from the same chart viewed during London or New York. The same pair can alternate between quiet consolidation, impulsive expansion, and news-driven instability as global activity shifts from one center to the next. When that rhythm is understood, volatility stops being something to fear blindly and becomes something to anticipate, filter, and use with greater discipline.

CHAPTER 2

Chapter 2: Building a Trader's Mindset and Trading Plan

Before a trader can judge a setup with discipline, there has to be a framework for judging the trader. That framework begins with expectations that are grounded in market reality rather than hope, with goals that match available time and temperament, and with a plan that defines what will be traded and how decisions will be made. Without that structure, even a sound method can be undermined by inconsistency, hesitation, or impulsive changes made in the heat of the moment. The purpose of this chapter is to shift the focus from reacting to price to organizing the process behind each trade, so that execution becomes deliberate instead of emotional.

Developing realistic expectations about profits, losses, and learning curves

Realistic expectations begin with accepting that forex trading is a business of probabilities, not predictions. A valid setup does not guarantee a profitable trade, and a losing trade does not automatically mean the method is flawed. What matters is whether the approach produces a positive edge over a meaningful sample of trades. That edge can be modest and still be valuable, because consistency comes from repeating sound decisions under controlled risk, not from trying to be right every time.

New traders often focus on how much they could make from a single trade or a single month. That mindset usually leads to distorted thinking. A better frame is to ask how much risk is being taken to pursue each opportunity, how often the setup appears, and what the strategy tends to produce across many trades. In practice, even strong methods can go through losing streaks. The market is not obligated to reward a good entry immediately, and a period of losses does not necessarily mean the trader lacks skill. It may simply reflect normal variation, changing conditions, or the limits of the strategy itself.

Learning curves are another area where unrealistic expectations cause damage. Progress in trading is rarely linear. Early improvement may come quickly as basic concepts become familiar, followed by a frustrating period where results stall or regress once live money is involved. That is not unusual. Executing a strategy in real time introduces pressure, hesitation, and emotional interference that do not appear in a chart example or a backtest. The trader is not only learning market behavior but also learning to manage attention, patience, and discipline under uncertainty.

It is also important to understand that a strategy can be technically sound and still fail in the wrong environment. Some methods perform better in trends, others in ranges, and many degrade when volatility changes abruptly. Research in trading systems and optimization consistently shows that models must be tested carefully and adapted to realistic conditions rather than assumed to work everywhere [6][43][20]. That same caution applies to discretionary trading. A setup that looked excellent during a favorable market phase may become unreliable when the market shifts. Realistic expectations include the possibility that part of the learning process is discovering when not to trade a method.

Another common mistake is measuring progress only by account balance. While profit and loss matter, they do not tell the full story. A trader can have a profitable month while violating risk rules, overtrading, or taking oversized positions that would not be sustainable over time. Likewise, a temporary drawdown does not automatically mean poor performance if the trader followed the plan and kept losses controlled. Better measures of progress include adherence to rules, average risk per trade, quality of execution, and whether the trader is making fewer avoidable mistakes than before.

Expectations should also account for the fact that the market changes faster than most traders do. A method that appears simple on paper may require months of repetition before it can be executed calmly and consistently. That is why it helps to define learning as a process with stages: understanding the setup, practicing recognition, applying it in a demo or small-risk environment, reviewing results, and refining execution. Skipping these stages usually creates a false sense of readiness. The objective is not to rush toward larger size, but to build enough evidence that the trader can trust the process when conditions become uncomfortable.

There is a useful distinction between being confident and being certain. Confidence comes from preparation, testing, and repetition. Certainty is dangerous because it encourages traders to ignore risk and assume the next trade will behave as expected. In forex, even high-quality signals can fail because of news, liquidity shifts, or broader market forces. A disciplined trader therefore expects uncertainty on every trade and plans for it in advance. That expectation does not weaken conviction; it makes conviction usable.

One practical way to keep expectations realistic is to think in terms of process goals rather than outcome goals. An outcome goal might be to double an account in a short period, but that target says little about the quality of the trading method or the trader's behavior. A process goal might be to risk a fixed percentage per trade, take only approved setups, and review every trade after the session. Process goals are more useful because they can be controlled directly. Over time, they create the conditions under which profitability becomes more likely, but they do not pretend that every week or every month will be smooth.

Defining trading goals, style, and time commitment

Defining your trading goals begins with being honest about what you want forex trading to do for you. Some traders are aiming to build a supplemental income stream, some want to develop a repeatable skill before committing serious capital, and some are looking for a longer-term path toward professional-level performance. Those are not the same objective, and they should not lead to the same expectations. A goal that is too vague, such as "make money trading," leaves too much room for emotional decision-making. A useful goal is specific enough to guide behavior, measurable enough to review, and realistic enough to survive normal losing periods. In practice, that means focusing on controllable outcomes first: how well you follow your rules, how consistently you manage risk, and how effectively you execute your process. Profits matter, but they are the result you evaluate after the process has been repeated over time.

It also helps to separate performance goals from process goals. A performance goal might be a target return over a quarter, but that number should never be the only standard you use to judge yourself. A process goal is more immediate and more useful: limit risk to a fixed percentage per trade, wait for setups that match your plan, and avoid trading during conditions you have defined as unfavorable. This distinction matters because the market does not reward effort in a straight line. A trader can do many things correctly and still experience a losing week or month. If your goals are built only around profit, normal variance can push you into frustration, overtrading, or abandoning a valid method too early. If your goals include execution quality, the focus stays on what you can control while the account equity develops over a larger sample.

Your trading style should follow from your temperament, not from what looks exciting on social media or in a highlight reel of fast wins. A trader who has a demanding day job, limited screen time, and a preference for calm decision-making may be better suited to swing trading than to active intraday scalping. Another trader may prefer the faster feedback of day trading, but only if they can remain focused, make decisions quickly, and accept that the pace will generate more noise and more opportunities for emotional error. There is no universal best style. The right style is the one that fits your personality, your patience level, and the way you naturally process information. If your method requires constant attention but your schedule only allows a few brief check-ins, the mismatch will eventually show up in poor execution.

Time commitment is one of the most overlooked parts of trader planning because the market is always open, but your attention is not. A realistic assessment of available time should include more than the minutes spent placing trades. You need time for chart review, news awareness, journaling, backtesting, and periodic performance analysis. A trader who plans to trade the London open, for example, must be available when that session is active and alert enough to make decisions without rushing. A swing trader may need less intraday screen time, but still needs enough time each day to monitor open positions and enough weekly time to review setups across multiple pairs. If you understate the time requirement, you create pressure to improvise. That pressure often leads to skipped preparation, late entries, and inconsistent risk management.

It is useful to define your trading schedule in concrete terms. Decide when you will analyze the market, when you will look for setups, and when you will stop trading for the day. A schedule creates boundaries, and boundaries reduce impulsive behavior. For some traders, that may mean reviewing charts in the evening and placing swing trades only once or twice a week. For others, it may mean a short pre-market scan, a defined trading window, and no additional trades after that window closes. The point is not to trade as often as possible. The point is to trade when your method has a genuine advantage and your attention is strong enough to apply it correctly. Over time, the discipline to stand aside is often as important as the discipline to enter.

The best way to align goals, style, and time commitment is to make them fit together as one structure. If your goal is steady skill development, your style should be simple enough to study and review, and your time commitment should leave room for learning rather than constant reaction. If your goal is to pursue shorter-term trading as a serious business, your style must be precise, repeatable, and supported by a schedule that allows for active monitoring and fast execution. If your available time is limited, you may need to reduce the number of pairs you follow, narrow the set of setups you trade, and accept a slower pace of account growth. That is not a weakness in the plan; it is what makes the plan workable.

One practical way to test whether your goals are properly matched to your circumstances is to ask a few direct questions before you commit to a method: How many hours per week can I reliably devote to trading and review? Do I want frequent decisions or fewer, higher-conviction decisions? Can I tolerate watching a trade move without interfering with it? Am I trying to build skill first, or am I trying to generate income immediately? Honest answers to those questions prevent a common mistake: adopting a trading style for its appeal rather than its fit. A style that matches your goals and your schedule gives you a better chance to stay consistent long enough for your edge, if you have one, to reveal itself.

Creating a personal trading plan with rules for entry, exit, and risk

A personal trading plan should turn your trading into a sequence of predefined decisions rather than a series of emotional reactions. If you do not know in advance what qualifies as a valid setup, where the trade will be exited, and how much capital is at risk, then the market will make those decisions for you. A written plan creates consistency. It also makes your results measurable, because you can compare what you did against what you intended to do. That comparison is essential if you want to improve in a disciplined way instead of simply repeating the same mistakes with different currency pairs.

The entry rules in a trading plan should be narrow enough to prevent random trades, but not so rigid that they ignore normal market variation. A good entry rule defines the conditions that must be present before you act. Those conditions may include trend direction, location relative to support or resistance, a candle pattern, a momentum confirmation, or a specific session window. The point is not to build a complicated checklist for its own sake. The point is to ensure that every trade is based on the same logic. When your entries are standardized, you reduce the temptation to chase price after it has already moved or to enter because a chart "looks good" without a clear reason.

It helps to separate a setup from a trigger. The setup is the broader market condition that makes a trade worth considering. The trigger is the final event that tells you to enter. For example, a setup might be a strong trend pulling back into a support zone, while the trigger might be a bullish rejection candle or a break of a short-term structure high. This distinction matters because it keeps you from entering too early. Many traders identify the right direction but still lose money because they act before the market confirms that buyers or sellers are actually stepping in. A plan that specifies both the setup and the trigger keeps you patient without making you passive.

Exit rules deserve the same level of precision as entries. Every trade should have a defined invalidation point, which is usually the stop-loss, and a profit objective or management rule for taking gains. The stop-loss should be placed where the trade idea is no longer valid, not at an arbitrary number of pips. That means the stop should reflect market structure, volatility, and the reason you entered in the first place. Profit exits can be based on a fixed target, a measured move, a key technical level, or a trailing method. What matters is that you decide before entry how the trade will be handled if it works and if it fails. Once the trade is live, your job is execution, not improvisation.

Risk rules are the part of the plan that protect you from the most damaging habits in trading. A common rule is to risk only a small, fixed percentage of account equity on each trade so that no single loss can do serious harm. That rule should be paired with a maximum daily or weekly loss limit, because even a good strategy can go through a rough stretch. If you keep trading after reaching a loss threshold, you often shift from disciplined decision-making to emotional recovery mode. A strong plan also defines how many positions you can hold at once, whether correlated pairs count as one combined exposure, and when trading should stop for the day. These limits are not signs of caution for its own sake; they are controls that keep a temporary setback from becoming a major drawdown.

Your plan should also state what market conditions are acceptable and which are not. Some strategies work best during active sessions, while others need calm conditions or clear trends. Some setups require normal spreads and liquid pairs; others should be avoided around major news releases because the risk of slippage and erratic movement is too high. By defining these filters in advance, you avoid forcing trades into poor conditions simply because your chart setup appears close to valid. This is where many traders weaken their own edge: they have a strategy, but they do not have rules for when the strategy should be put aside.

A useful trading plan is written in language that can be checked after the fact. If a rule cannot be tested against a chart or a trade record, it is too vague. "Good momentum," "strong trend," and "safe entry" are not enough unless you define what those terms mean in practice. Your plan should be specific enough that another trader could look at the same chart and understand whether the rules were followed. That level of clarity makes journaling more useful, because you can identify whether a loss came from a valid trade, a poor execution, or a rule violation. Over time, that distinction is what allows you to refine the method instead of blaming the market for every setback.

A practical plan is not meant to be perfect on paper before you ever trade. It is meant to be usable, repeatable, and strict enough to keep you out of avoidable trouble. Many traders improve not by finding a magical entry signal, but by making their rules simpler, clearer, and more consistent. The fewer decisions you have to invent in real time, the less room there is for hesitation, overconfidence, or revenge trading. A well-built plan does not remove uncertainty from forex trading, but it does define how you will respond to uncertainty with discipline.

Common psychological traps: overconfidence, fear, revenge trading, and impatience

The most dangerous psychological mistakes in trading are rarely dramatic on their own. They usually begin as small distortions in judgment: a trader feels unusually confident after a winning streak, hesitates after a few losses, tries to "win it back" after a bad trade, or forces a setup because waiting feels uncomfortable. These behaviors matter because they interfere with the one advantage a trader can actually control: the consistency of decision-making. A strategy may have a valid edge, but that edge can be erased if the trader keeps changing behavior from one emotional state to another.

Overconfidence often appears after a period of success, especially when a trader starts to believe that recent results reflect skill more than favorable conditions. This can lead to larger position sizes, looser entry standards, or the assumption that the market will continue to behave the same way it has in the recent past. The problem is not confidence itself; a trader needs enough confidence to execute a plan without second-guessing every trade. The problem is inflated confidence that becomes a substitute for analysis. When that happens, the trader stops respecting risk and begins treating a good run as proof that discipline is no longer necessary. Markets punish that assumption quickly, because conditions shift whether a trader is ready or not.

Fear is the opposite distortion, but it can be just as costly. After a string of losses, or even after one trade that was emotionally difficult, a trader may begin to doubt valid signals and hesitate at the moment of execution. Fear can show up as premature exits, reduced position sizes that are inconsistent with the plan, or complete avoidance of trades that meet the criteria. In many cases the trader is not afraid of the market itself so much as afraid of being wrong again. That fear narrows attention and encourages defensive behavior that may feel safe but often destroys the statistical value of the system. A well-defined plan exists partly to reduce this kind of emotional interference by making the decision before the pressure of the live trade arrives.

Revenge trading is one of the clearest signs that a trader has shifted from process to emotion. It usually follows a loss that feels unfair, avoidable, or personally frustrating. Instead of accepting the loss as part of normal variance, the trader tries to recover immediately by entering a new trade without proper confirmation, increasing size to "make back" the damage, or abandoning normal filters in search of quick redemption. The danger is not just the added risk on the next trade; it is the collapse of judgment that comes with it. A revenge trade is rarely a response to the market. It is a response to discomfort. Once discomfort becomes the reason for action, the trader is no longer following a strategy but reacting to emotional pressure.

Impatience is more subtle, but it can undermine performance over time just as effectively. A trader may know the setup requirements and still enter too early because waiting feels unproductive. Impatience also appears when a trader forces trades in slow market conditions, chases price after missing an entry, or constantly changes time frames in search of action. This behavior often comes from confusing activity with progress. In reality, trading is not improved by being busy; it is improved by being selective. The willingness to wait for a valid setup is part of the edge. Without that patience, even a sound method becomes diluted by low-quality entries.

These traps often feed one another. Overconfidence can make a trader ignore risk, a loss can trigger fear, fear can lead to hesitation, hesitation can create frustration, and frustration can lead to revenge trading or impatience. That cycle is why psychological control cannot be treated as a vague matter of "staying calm." It has to be built into the trading process. Clear rules for entry, exit, and risk are important not only because they organize the trade, but because they reduce the number of moments in which emotion can override judgment. The less room there is for improvisation, the less opportunity there is for psychological drift.

One useful discipline is to identify which trap tends to appear first for you. Some traders become overconfident after a few wins and start relaxing standards. Others become fearful after losses and begin avoiding valid opportunities. Some are especially vulnerable to revenge trading because they hate giving money back to the market. Others struggle most with impatience and enter before the market has actually confirmed the setup. Recognizing the pattern matters because each trap requires a different correction. Overconfidence calls for tighter adherence to size limits and checklist discipline. Fear calls for restoring trust in the process. Revenge trading calls for a pause between loss and re-entry. Impatience calls for stricter waiting rules and fewer discretionary exceptions.

Psychological control is not about eliminating emotion, because that is not realistic. It is about preventing emotion from becoming the decision-maker. A trader who can notice the first signs of overconfidence, fear, revenge, or impatience has already gained an important edge over the trader who only notices the damage after the trade is closed. The goal is to make emotional states visible early enough that they can be managed before they alter the plan. That habit becomes part of professionalism: not the absence of pressure, but the ability to keep trading decisions inside a structure that remains stable when pressure rises.

CHAPTER 3

Chapter 3: Reading Price Action and Market Structure

Once the trader's plan is in place, the next task is learning to read what price is actually doing instead of relying on assumptions about what it should do. Price action and market structure give you that context by showing how buyers and sellers are responding in real time, where momentum is building or fading, and whether the market is behaving in a way that supports a trade idea. This is not about predicting every turn; it is about recognizing the conditions that tend to precede continuation, hesitation, or change.

Candlestick basics and what individual bars reveal about market sentiment

Candlesticks condense a battle between buyers and sellers into a single visual unit. Each bar shows four key pieces of information: the open, high, low, and close. The body marks the distance between the open and close, while the wicks show how far price traveled beyond that body during the period. That simple structure makes candlesticks more informative than a line chart because they reveal not only where price ended, but also how it behaved while getting there. A trader who reads them well is not trying to memorize shapes in isolation; the goal is to understand what the bar says about control, rejection, and commitment.

The most basic distinction is between a bullish and bearish close. When the close finishes above the open, the candle is bullish; when it closes below the open, it is bearish. But the color alone is not enough to judge sentiment. A strong bullish candle with a large body and little upper wick suggests buyers were able to keep pressure on price through the period. A bearish candle with a large body and little lower wick suggests sellers maintained control. By contrast, a candle with a small body and long wicks on both sides often signals indecision or a temporary balance between opposing forces. In other words, the market is not always trending or reversing with conviction; sometimes it is simply pausing while participants reassess value.

The size of the body matters because it reflects the degree of commitment behind the move. A wide body usually indicates that price traveled efficiently from open to close, which can be a sign of momentum. A narrow body suggests hesitation, compression, or a lack of follow-through. That does not automatically make the narrow candle unimportant. In a trend, a small candle can show a brief rest before continuation. Near support or resistance, it can show that the market is struggling to accept higher or lower prices. The key is to read the bar in context. A candle that looks weak in one location may be meaningful in another because the surrounding structure changes what the market is likely trying to do.

Wicks are especially useful because they show rejection. A long upper wick tells you price was pushed higher but could not hold those gains by the close. That often suggests supply entered the market at the higher level. A long lower wick tells you price was pushed lower but buyers stepped in and forced a recovery. That can indicate demand at the lower level. Rejection is not the same thing as reversal, but it is often the first clue that a level matters. If repeated candles show the same area producing long wicks, the market is telling you that participants are defending that zone. Traders who ignore wicks often miss the subtle evidence of where order flow is changing.

Single candles are useful, but clusters of candles tell a more complete story. A strong candle followed by another strong candle in the same direction suggests follow-through and sustained interest. A strong candle followed by several small candles can suggest the move is losing energy. Likewise, a candle that breaks a recent high or low but closes back inside the prior range may show a failed attempt to continue. That kind of failure can be more informative than a clean breakout because it reveals that the market tested a level and was pushed back. In practice, many useful price-action decisions come from noticing whether the current candle confirms the previous one or contradicts it.

Location gives the candle its real meaning. A bullish candle in the middle of a choppy range does not carry the same weight as a bullish candle breaking above a well-tested resistance area. A bearish candle after an extended rally may simply be normal profit-taking, while the same candle at a major swing high could signal that buyers are losing control. This is why candlestick analysis should never be reduced to pattern recognition alone. A pin bar, engulfing candle, or rejection wick is not a signal by itself; it becomes more relevant when it appears at a location where the market has already shown sensitivity. The bar is the message, but the chart structure is the context.

It also helps to think about candles as evidence of imbalance rather than certainty. A large bullish candle does not guarantee higher prices next; it only shows that buyers won the current period decisively. A long lower wick does not guarantee a reversal; it shows that selling pressure was absorbed at least temporarily. This distinction matters because traders often confuse a readable candle with a predictable outcome. Candlestick reading is strongest when it helps you frame probability, not when it is used to force a forecast. Some research on trading systems design also emphasizes that individual signals are more effective when evaluated as part of a broader decision process rather than treated as stand-alone predictions [73].

For a forex trader, the practical habit is to ask a few disciplined questions every time a candle closes: Did price close near the high or low of the bar? Was the body large or small relative to recent candles? Were the wicks showing rejection, hesitation, or both? And most importantly, where did this happen in relation to the recent structure? Those questions keep the focus on sentiment and participation instead of on chart decoration. Over time, this way of reading individual bars helps you see whether the market is expanding, stalling, accepting a new price area, or rejecting it. That is the real value of candlestick analysis: it turns each bar into a compact record of how the market is thinking right now.

Trend identification, support and resistance, and market structure shifts

Trend identification begins with the simple question of whether price is making progress in one direction or merely oscillating around a level. In an uptrend, higher highs and higher lows show that buyers are willing to pay progressively more, while in a downtrend lower highs and lower lows show that sellers are controlling the path of least resistance. That sounds obvious, but the practical challenge is that trends are rarely clean on the lower time frames. A trader has to distinguish between a real directional move and a temporary burst of volatility inside a larger sideways structure. The most reliable way to do that is to look at swing points, not individual candles. A sequence of rising swing lows and rising swing highs carries more meaning than a few strong bullish bars, because it shows that the market is accepting higher prices over time.

Support and resistance are best treated as zones rather than exact lines. Price does not respect a single pip level with mathematical precision; it reacts to areas where buying or selling previously became active enough to change direction. A support zone is an area where demand has repeatedly appeared, slowing or reversing declines. Resistance is the opposite, where supply has been strong enough to stall advances. These areas matter because they represent memory in the market. Traders remember where price previously turned, and order flow often clusters around those same regions again. A level becomes more meaningful when it has been tested more than once, when the reactions are decisive, and when the move away from the level is strong enough to show that participation was real rather than random.

It is also important to separate reaction from confirmation. Price may touch support and bounce, but that does not automatically mean the level will hold on the next test. The market often probes beyond obvious levels to trigger resting orders, stop losses, or breakout entries before deciding whether to continue. That is why traders should focus on how price behaves when it reaches a zone. Does it reject the level quickly with strong momentum? Does it stall and form smaller candles, suggesting indecision? Does it close decisively through the area and then retest it from the other side? These details matter more than the label attached to the line on the chart. A level that fails cleanly can be just as useful as a level that holds, because failure often reveals a shift in who is in control.

Market structure shifts are the moment when the existing pattern of highs and lows changes in a way that suggests the prior trend may be weakening or reversing. In an uptrend, the first warning sign is often a failure to make a new high followed by a break below the most recent higher low. In a downtrend, the warning sign is a failure to make a new low followed by a break above the most recent lower high. This does not mean the trend is instantly over, but it does mean the market has stopped behaving in the same way. A true structure shift is more convincing when the break is followed by acceptance on the other side of the level rather than a fast snap back. In other words, the market should not only pierce the level; it should begin to trade as if that level has changed roles.

That role change is one of the most useful concepts in price action. Former resistance can become support after a breakout, and former support can become resistance after a breakdown. Traders often call this a retest, but the deeper idea is acceptance. When price breaks through an area and then returns to it without reclaiming the old side, it suggests that market participants now view the zone differently. This is one reason many traders prefer to wait for the retest instead of chasing the initial break. The retest helps confirm whether the breakout was supported by enough participation to hold. In practice, this can reduce false entries, especially in markets that are prone to sharp intraday spikes and reversals.

One mistake traders make is treating support and resistance as isolated technical facts rather than expressions of the broader structure. A level that appears important on the 15-minute chart may be insignificant on the four-hour chart if it sits inside a larger trend leg. For that reason, structure should always be read in context. The higher time frame shows the larger path, while the lower time frame helps refine the timing. If the daily chart is still making higher highs and higher lows, a short-term pullback into support is more likely to be a continuation opportunity than a major reversal. If the larger structure has already broken, the same pullback may simply be a retest before further decline. Multi-time-frame alignment is not about finding more signals; it is about understanding which signals are working with the dominant flow and which are fighting it.

There is also a discipline issue here: traders should avoid forcing labels onto every chart. Not every pause is a range, not every breakout is meaningful, and not every shift in momentum is a structural reversal. Good structure reading is patient and selective. It asks whether price has actually changed its behavior or merely paused within the same behavior. That distinction becomes clearer when you compare the size and speed of swings, the location of closes relative to key zones, and the market's willingness to continue after a break. Technical research across forecasting methods continues to show that pattern recognition can support decision-making, but only when the trader applies it with context and discipline rather than treating it as a shortcut to prediction [74][18].

Breakouts, pullbacks, consolidations, and reversal signals

Price action often leaves its clearest clues at the edges of a move, where momentum either expands into a breakout or fades into a pause. A breakout occurs when price pushes beyond a well-defined barrier, such as resistance in an uptrend or support in a downtrend, and then proves that the move is more than a brief probe. The key distinction is not simply that price crossed a level, but that it did so with enough conviction to attract follow-through. Traders who mistake every temporary poke through a level for a breakout usually discover that the market is not obligated to continue just because a line on the chart was touched. A valid breakout is typically easier to trust when it comes after a period of compression, such as a narrow range, a tightening triangle, or a series of smaller candles that suggest energy is building.

Not every breakout should be traded the same way. Some are continuation breakouts, where price exits a pause and resumes the prevailing trend. Others are reversal breakouts, where a major level gives way and the market begins a new directional phase. In both cases, the trader should look for evidence that the move is being accepted rather than rejected. Acceptance can appear as a strong close beyond the level, a follow-through candle, or a sustained inability to trade back inside the prior range. The more time price spends trying to reclaim the broken level, the more likely the move is losing force. Breakouts that happen during thin liquidity or just ahead of major news deserve extra caution because the move may be exaggerated by temporary order flow rather than supported by broader participation.

Pullbacks are the market's way of testing commitment. After a strong move, price often retraces part of the advance before deciding whether to continue. For trend traders, this is often a better entry point than chasing the initial impulse because the pullback can offer a more favorable price and a clearer risk reference. The challenge is to distinguish a healthy retracement from a genuine reversal. A healthy pullback usually corrects in a controlled way, often staying within the structure of the trend and failing to break the sequence of higher lows in an uptrend or lower highs in a downtrend. When the retracement becomes deeper, more erratic, or starts closing decisively beyond prior swing points, the trader should question whether the original trend is still intact.

Consolidations deserve special attention because they are the market's pause between decisions. During consolidation, price moves sideways or within a relatively tight band as buyers and sellers reach temporary balance. This is not dead time; it is often a period of accumulation, distribution, or simply indecision before the next expansion. Traders should avoid assuming that a consolidation is automatically a base for continuation. Some ranges resolve in the direction of the prior trend, but others become reversal zones because the market uses the pause to absorb the earlier move and build pressure in the opposite direction. The quality of the boundaries matters. A clean range with repeated reactions at support and resistance is more useful than a messy cluster of overlapping candles with no clear structure.

Reversal signals are most reliable when they appear at meaningful locations, not in the middle of random price noise. A single candlestick pattern is rarely enough on its own. What matters is context: where the signal appears, what trend preceded it, and whether momentum has already begun to weaken. Signs of reversal can include failure to make a new high or low, repeated rejection of a level, a sharp shift in candle size or direction, or a break in market structure after an extended move. For example, if an uptrend starts producing weaker pushes, then stalls at resistance, then breaks a prior higher low, the market is telling you that buyers may no longer be in control. The same logic applies in reverse for a downtrend. Reversal signals gain credibility when they are confirmed by a break of structure rather than treated as a prediction based on one candle alone.

The practical task is to separate signal from noise. Many traders lose discipline by reacting to the first sign of movement instead of waiting for confirmation. Confirmation does not mean waiting so long that the trade becomes unattractive; it means demanding enough evidence that the market has shown its hand. A breakout may need a close beyond the level and a retest that holds. A pullback may need to stabilize near a trend boundary before entry. A consolidation may need a clear expansion candle with follow-through. A reversal may need a failure swing and then a structural break. The exact rule depends on the trading plan, but the principle is the same: let price prove that the move has enough participation to matter. This is one reason disciplined decision making matters so much in retail trading, where reacting to shifting conditions without a clear method often undermines performance [40].

These patterns are most useful when they are read in sequence rather than in isolation. A trend often begins with a breakout, pauses in a pullback, rests in a consolidation, and then either resumes or reverses. If you can identify which phase the market is in, you are less likely to force the wrong strategy onto the chart. Breakouts favor momentum thinking, pullbacks favor patience and precision, consolidations favor restraint until expansion appears, and reversal signals demand skepticism toward the old trend. The goal is not to predict which pattern will appear next, but to recognize what the market is already expressing and to respond with a trade plan that matches that expression.

Using multiple time frames to improve context and decision-making

Using multiple time frames is one of the simplest ways to keep a chart from lying to you. A single chart compresses market behavior into one perspective, and that perspective can be misleading if it is treated as the whole story. The lower time frame may show a clean entry pattern, but if the higher time frame is still trapped inside broad resistance, the trade is being taken against a larger force. Likewise, a weekly chart may suggest a strong trend, while the intraday chart reveals that price is extended and vulnerable to a pullback. The point is not to find a “perfect” chart; it is to align the narrower view with the broader one so that your decisions are based on context rather than noise.

A practical way to think about multiple time frames is to assign each one a job. The higher time frame provides the directional bias and the major structure. It tells you whether the market is trending, ranging, or transitioning, and where the important boundaries are likely to sit. The middle time frame helps refine the trade idea by showing the active swing structure, the most recent reaction highs and lows, and the areas where price is likely to pause or accelerate. The lower time frame is where execution happens. It should be used to time entries, manage risk, and avoid entering blindly into a poor location. When each time frame has a defined purpose, the chart becomes a decision framework instead of a collection of conflicting signals.

This approach works best when the time frames are related rather than random. A trader who uses the daily chart for bias, the four-hour chart for setup, and the one-hour chart for entry is usually looking at a coherent sequence. The daily chart may show that price is making higher highs and higher lows, which suggests that buyers still have control. The four-hour chart may then reveal a pullback into prior support or a consolidation near a breakout level. The one-hour chart can then be used to look for evidence that the pullback is ending, such as a rejection candle, a minor structure break, or a clean retest. In this sequence, the lower time frame is not leading the analysis; it is confirming a trade idea that already fits the larger structure.

The danger comes when traders let the lowest time frame dominate their judgment. A one-minute or five-minute chart can produce constant movement, but much of that movement is simply microstructure noise. A brief spike, a fast reversal, or a sharp candle may look like a meaningful signal when viewed in isolation, yet it may be nothing more than routine fluctuation inside a larger range. Traders who focus too narrowly often enter late, exit too early, or reverse positions too quickly because they are reacting to every small change in price. The higher time frame helps filter that noise. It tells you whether the move you are seeing has the room to continue or whether it is likely to stall into a larger barrier.

Multiple time frame analysis is especially useful around support and resistance, trend transitions, and breakout conditions. A level that appears minor on a lower chart may be far more important on a higher one. For example, a breakout on the one-hour chart may be meaningless if price is still below a weekly resistance zone. On the other hand, a pullback on the lower chart can become an attractive entry if it is taking place inside a larger uptrend and near a higher-time-frame support area. This layered view also helps with stop placement. Stops placed too tightly against lower-time-frame noise are often vulnerable, while stops placed without regard to the broader structure may be unnecessarily large. The best placement usually reflects both the entry chart and the larger chart structure.

The same logic applies to trade management. If the higher time frame still supports the move, a lower-time-frame pullback may be a normal pause rather than a reason to exit. If the broader structure is weakening, however, a lower-time-frame bounce may be little more than temporary relief. This is where multiple time frames protect traders from emotional overreaction. Instead of asking, "Did the last candle move against me?" the better question is, "Does this movement change the larger setup?" That shift in perspective improves discipline because it reduces the tendency to micromanage every fluctuation. It also helps traders hold winning positions long enough to benefit from the move they originally identified.

It is also important not to overload the analysis with too many time frames. More charts do not automatically mean better decisions. In practice, three related time frames are usually enough: one for context, one for setup, and one for execution. Too many layers can create analysis paralysis, especially if each chart is given equal weight. The goal is consistency. A trader should know in advance which chart defines the trend, which chart defines the setup, and which chart triggers the entry. Once that structure is established, the market becomes easier to interpret because each time frame contributes a specific piece of information rather than competing for attention.

CHAPTER 4

Chapter 4: Technical Analysis Tools That Improve Trade Decisions

Technical analysis tools are most useful when they help a trader reduce uncertainty, not when they are treated as prediction machines. The market rarely offers a single obvious clue, so the value of indicators and pattern tools lies in how they organize price behavior, highlight momentum shifts, and support a decision that already makes sense within the broader market context. Used well, they can improve timing and discipline; used poorly, they can create noise, delay action, or encourage traders to see signals that are not really there. That distinction matters because forex trading rewards clear judgment more than crowded charts.

Moving averages, oscillators, and momentum indicators: strengths and limitations

Moving averages are among the most useful tools for organizing price behavior because they smooth out some of the noise that makes raw charts hard to read. A simple moving average can help define the direction of the prevailing move, while a faster average can show whether price is accelerating or losing pace. In practice, traders often use them to filter setups rather than to generate them on their own. For example, a rising average may support long trades in an uptrend, but that does not mean every pullback is a buy. The value of the tool is contextual: it helps a trader see whether the market is trending, ranging, or transitioning, and that context can improve discipline more than it improves prediction.

The main limitation of moving averages is that they are derived from past prices, so they always lag. That lag is not a flaw so much as a tradeoff, but it matters. By the time a moving average confirms a trend change, a meaningful portion of the move may already be complete. This is especially true in fast forex conditions, where news, session changes, and liquidity shifts can produce sharp moves before any lagging indicator has time to catch up. Crossovers between moving averages can be helpful as a visual cue, but they often arrive late and can produce a string of false signals when the market is choppy. A crossover that looks clean on a chart may simply reflect temporary volatility rather than a durable shift in control.

Oscillators such as RSI and stochastic are designed to help traders judge whether price is stretched, weakening, or potentially ready for a pause. Their strength is that they can highlight momentum conditions that are not obvious from price alone. In a range, an oscillator can be especially useful for identifying overextended moves near support or resistance, where a reversal or retracement is more likely. These tools can also help a trader notice when price is still making new highs or lows but the oscillator is failing to confirm that strength, which may signal fading momentum. Used carefully, oscillators can improve timing by showing when a market is moving too far, too fast, or with less internal force than the chart first suggests.

Their weakness is that they can tempt traders into treating overbought and oversold readings as automatic reversal signals. In a strong trend, an oscillator can remain elevated or depressed for a long time while price continues in the same direction. That is why these readings should never be used in isolation. An overbought RSI in an uptrend does not automatically mean sell; it may simply mean the market is strong. Likewise, oversold conditions in a downtrend can persist while sellers remain in control. Research on trading systems and financial forecasting repeatedly shows that indicator performance depends heavily on market regime and parameter choice, and that no single formula is reliably superior across all conditions [89][95]. That is a useful reminder that oscillator signals are best treated as context, not command.

Momentum indicators occupy a middle ground between trend-following tools and oscillators. They attempt to measure the speed or persistence of price movement, which can be useful when a trader wants to know whether a breakout has genuine force behind it. If price is pushing through a level and momentum is expanding with it, the move has a better chance of follow-through than if price is creeping forward with weak participation. Momentum tools can also be used to compare one phase of the market with another, helping a trader distinguish a healthy trend from one that is tiring. In that sense, they are often most valuable as confirmation tools rather than as stand-alone entry signals.

The limitation is that momentum can disappear quickly, especially in forex, where liquidity changes across sessions and major releases can abruptly alter behavior. A momentum reading that looks strong during one time window may fade as soon as market participation thins or opposing flows enter. This is one reason many data-driven studies emphasize that forecasting exchange-rate behavior remains difficult and that indicators alone do not solve the problem of unstable financial conditions [90][91][92]. Even advanced models that combine technical inputs with other data still face the challenge of changing regimes, which is a reminder that no indicator removes uncertainty from the market. The goal is not to find certainty; it is to improve odds.

A practical way to use these tools is to assign each one a job. A moving average can define trend and structure, an oscillator can warn of stretched conditions, and a momentum indicator can help judge whether a move has strength or is merely drifting. When all three point in the same general direction, the case for a trade becomes stronger. When they conflict, that disagreement is often a signal to slow down rather than to force a decision. The most common mistake is indicator overload, where a chart becomes crowded with overlapping signals that say nearly the same thing in different ways. A cleaner approach is usually better: one or two tools that support the logic of the trade, combined with price action and market structure, will usually outperform a cluttered screen full of redundant confirmation.

Chart patterns and how to validate them with price action

Chart patterns are useful because they translate repeated shifts in crowd behavior into recognizable structures. A double top, head and shoulders, triangle, flag, or range is not valuable simply because it has a name; it is valuable because it reflects a phase in which buyers and sellers are interacting in a measurable way. The mistake many traders make is treating the pattern itself as the signal. In practice, the pattern is only the setup framework. The real question is whether price is behaving in a way that confirms the pattern's logic. That confirmation comes from price action: the strength or weakness of the swings, the quality of the breakout, the way price reacts at key levels, and whether the market follows through after the initial move.

Validation begins with context. A pattern that forms in the middle of congestion has less meaning than one that appears after a clear trend, at a well-defined support or resistance zone, or at a point where momentum has already begun to change. For example, a bullish flag is more credible when it develops after a sharp impulsive advance, because the pause looks like temporary profit-taking rather than random noise. A head and shoulders top carries more weight when the left shoulder, head, and right shoulder show a gradual loss of buying pressure and the neckline aligns with an obvious structural level. The pattern should fit the surrounding market behavior, not stand apart from it. If the broader structure does not support the idea, the pattern is weaker no matter how tidy it appears.

Price action confirmation usually shows up in the candles around the pattern boundaries. When price approaches resistance and repeatedly fails to close above it, the market is telling you that buyers are not yet strong enough to overcome supply. When a breakout finally occurs, the quality of that breakout matters more than the fact that it happened. Strong validation often includes a decisive candle body, limited wick rejection against the breakout direction, and a close beyond the level rather than a brief intraday poke through it. In contrast, a breakout that immediately stalls, reverses, or closes back inside the pattern often signals that the move was not accepted by the market. That is especially important in forex, where liquidity can create short-lived spikes that look convincing until the session closes.

One of the most reliable ways to validate a pattern is to wait for retest behavior. After a breakout, former resistance should ideally act as support in a bullish move, and former support should act as resistance in a bearish move. That change in role is a practical sign that the market has accepted the new direction. A clean retest does not have to be perfect, but it should show that the level is being respected rather than immediately reclaimed. If price breaks out and then returns to the level with smaller candles, reduced momentum, or clear rejection wicks, the pattern has stronger confirmation than if price slices back through the level with force. This is why many traders prefer to trade the retest rather than the initial break: it provides a clearer read on whether the market is truly committed.

Volume can help, but in spot forex it is usually interpreted through tick volume and should be used as supporting evidence rather than proof. A breakout accompanied by expanding activity is generally more convincing than one that occurs on thin participation, especially if the move happens during a major session overlap. Still, the most important confirmation remains price itself. If a pattern is valid, the market should behave consistently with the story the pattern implies. A bullish continuation pattern should show higher lows holding on pullbacks. A bearish reversal should show rallies losing momentum and failing to reclaim prior highs. If price is making the opposite kind of behavior, the pattern is probably not ready or may be failing outright.

False patterns are common because traders often identify shapes before the market has finished deciding what they mean. A rectangle can become a continuation pattern, a reversal pattern, or simply a pause before another range. A triangle can resolve in either direction, and the first break is not always the final answer. This is why validation should include a sequence of questions rather than a single trigger: Did the pattern form at a meaningful level? Did price reject the opposite side cleanly? Did the breakout close with conviction? Did the retest hold? Did follow-through continue beyond the initial burst? The more of these conditions that align, the more confidence a trader can have that the pattern is acting as intended.

It also helps to compare the pattern against the time frame above it. A pattern that looks attractive on an hourly chart may be running directly into a weekly resistance zone, which reduces its odds of success. Likewise, a small reversal pattern inside a larger trend may only be a temporary pause. Higher-time-frame structure gives the pattern a frame of reference, while lower-time-frame price action helps refine entry and risk. This layered approach is especially useful for forex traders because the market can move sharply within sessions while still respecting broader directional pressure. A pattern that aligns with the larger trend and shows clean candle confirmation at the entry level is materially stronger than one that appears isolated from the bigger picture.

The practical discipline is to treat patterns as hypotheses, not certainties. A setup becomes tradable when price action confirms that the market is behaving in line with the pattern's expectation. That means waiting for evidence, not anticipation, and being willing to pass on patterns that look textbook but fail to show acceptance, rejection, or follow-through. Traders who learn to validate patterns this way avoid many of the traps that come from pattern recognition alone. The chart may suggest an idea, but price action decides whether that idea deserves capital.

Volume, volatility, and confirmation tools for better trade timing

Volume is one of the most practical context tools a forex trader can use, but it has to be handled carefully because spot forex does not trade on one centralized exchange. That means there is no single, complete volume figure for the entire market. Instead, traders usually work with tick volume, which measures how often price changes during a period rather than the exact number of contracts traded. While it is not perfect, tick volume can still be useful because active markets tend to produce more frequent price updates, and that activity often lines up with stronger participation and cleaner follow-through. The key is not to treat volume as a standalone signal, but as a way to judge whether a move has real interest behind it or is simply drifting on thin participation.

In practice, volume is most helpful when it confirms price behavior at important levels. A breakout through resistance, for example, has more credibility if it expands on noticeably higher activity than the bars that came before it. That does not guarantee continuation, but it suggests that more participants are engaged and that the move may have enough energy to extend. By contrast, a breakout that occurs on weak activity can be a warning that the market is probing a level without broad commitment. The same idea applies to pullbacks. If price retraces on lighter activity inside an established trend, the move may be a temporary pause rather than a true shift in control. If the retracement is accompanied by expanding activity and stronger rejection candles, the market may be doing more than resting.

Volume also helps traders interpret exhaustion. A strong trend can continue for a long time, but it often loses quality before it reverses. When price keeps pushing into new territory while volume fails to expand, the market may be stretching beyond its current participation base. That matters because a move can remain visually impressive even as its internal strength weakens. In this setting, a trader is not trying to predict a reversal just because volume is fading. The goal is more modest: to recognize when the market is becoming less efficient and when chasing late entries carries more risk. Volume, then, is less about finding the exact turning point and more about understanding whether the latest push is being supported or merely extended by inertia.

Volatility serves a different function. If volume asks whether the market is participating, volatility asks how far price is willing to travel. A pair with low volatility may still trend, but it may take longer to reach a target and may require tighter expectations for profit. A pair with high volatility can create faster opportunities, but it also increases the chance of wider swings, deeper pullbacks, and stop-outs that occur before the trade has time to work. This is why volatility should influence both entry timing and risk placement. A stop that makes sense in a quiet market may be too tight during a news-driven expansion, while a wide stop in a calm market may expose the trader to unnecessary loss. Volatility measures such as average true range can help translate market behavior into practical trade planning, especially when deciding whether a setup offers enough room to justify the risk.

Confirmation tools are most valuable when they reduce the chance of acting on a single misleading clue. A price level may look important, but an experienced trader wants to see whether the market accepts that level, rejects it, or repeatedly tests it without commitment. Confirmation can come from several places: a closing price that holds beyond a breakout level, a momentum indicator that supports the direction of the move, a retest that respects prior resistance as new support, or a clear shift in candle behavior after the initial push. The point is not to stack every possible tool on the chart. It is to require enough agreement that the trade idea is based on evidence rather than excitement. Technical analysis research has long treated price behavior as a legitimate basis for identifying opportunities, while also showing that no single method is universally reliable across all conditions [54][86].

A useful way to think about confirmation is to separate setup from trigger. The setup is the broader condition that makes a trade worth watching, such as a trend, range boundary, or breakout structure. The trigger is the specific evidence that the market is behaving in the expected way right now. For example, a trader may identify a bullish structure on the higher time frame, then wait for a lower time frame pullback to stall on lighter activity and produce a strong rejection candle before entering. That sequence prevents the trader from buying simply because price is near a level. It also creates a more disciplined decision process, because the trade is only taken when the market shows that buyers are still active at the point of decision. This approach is particularly useful in fast conditions, where price can look convincing for only a short time before reversing.

The best confirmation tools are the ones that fit the market environment. In a quiet session, a modest expansion in activity and a clean close beyond a level may be enough. In a volatile session, especially around major data releases, the same pattern may be too unstable to trust without additional evidence. Traders who adapt their confirmation standards to current conditions are less likely to be shaken out by noise or trapped by false moves. That is especially important in forex, where liquidity can shift quickly across sessions and where price can accelerate sharply when order flow becomes one-sided [103][105]. Used well, volume, volatility, and confirmation do not remove uncertainty. They make uncertainty more manageable by helping the trader distinguish between a market that is merely moving and a market that is actually committing.

Avoiding indicator overload and building a clean, repeatable chart setup

Indicator overload usually begins with good intentions. A trader wants confirmation, so one indicator is added. Then another is added to filter false signals, then a third to time entries, then a fourth to manage exits. Before long, the chart is crowded with overlapping tools that all measure some variation of the same thing. The result is not better analysis but slower decisions, more hesitation, and a greater chance of seeing what you want to see. In forex, where price can move quickly and conditions can change within a single session, a cluttered chart often creates the illusion of precision while reducing actual clarity.

The core problem is redundancy. Many indicators are built from the same underlying data: price. Moving averages, oscillators, momentum tools, and volatility measures can all be useful, but they often respond to the same market move in different ways. If three tools are all telling you that the market is trending, you do not have three independent confirmations; you usually have one trend observation repeated in three formats. That repetition can make a setup feel stronger than it really is. A cleaner approach is to ask what each tool contributes that the others do not. If an indicator does not add a distinct layer of information, it is probably noise.

A practical chart setup starts with price itself. That means candles, structure, and the levels that matter most to the current trade idea. From there, add only a small number of tools that serve a specific purpose. One common framework is a trend filter, a momentum or timing tool, and a volatility or range reference. For example, a moving average can help define the prevailing direction, an oscillator can help avoid entering after an extended move, and an average true range or similar measure can help judge whether the market has room to move. The point is not to build a universal template for every market condition. The point is to create a repeatable framework that answers the same questions every time you open a chart.

Repeatability matters because it reduces decision fatigue. When every trade is analyzed with a different combination of indicators, the trader is forced to reinterpret the market from scratch. That invites inconsistency. A stable chart layout, by contrast, trains your eye to notice meaningful changes faster. You begin to recognize when price is respecting structure, when momentum is weakening, and when volatility is expanding enough to support a trade. Over time, this consistency is more valuable than constantly searching for a new technical edge. Research on trading systems and market prediction has repeatedly shown that model design and feature selection matter, but complexity alone does not guarantee better performance [3][67].

One useful discipline is to separate setup tools from decision tools. Setup tools help you identify conditions worth watching, such as trend direction, support and resistance, or a consolidation that may lead to expansion. Decision tools help you choose whether the trade is valid now, such as a candle close beyond a level or a pullback into a preferred area. If an indicator is being asked to do both jobs at once, it often becomes less reliable. A moving average crossover, for instance, may help define bias, but it is rarely the best standalone trigger. A stochastic or RSI reading may help avoid chasing an extended move, but it should not override obvious price structure. Each tool should have a narrow, clearly defined role.

It also helps to think in terms of market regime. A clean chart setup for a trending pair does not need to be the same as a setup for a range-bound pair. In a trend, a trader may rely on structure, a directional filter, and a simple pullback trigger. In a range, the same tools may produce misleading signals unless they are adjusted for the environment. This is one reason traders get into trouble when they force a single indicator package onto every market condition. The better habit is to build a small menu of approved setups, each with a defined context, entry trigger, stop placement logic, and invalidation rule. That way, the chart is not telling you everything; it is telling you only what matters for the current type of trade.

Visual simplicity is part of risk control as well. A crowded chart can tempt a trader to overtrade because it creates the feeling that more information means more opportunity. In practice, the opposite is often true. The more signals you track, the more likely you are to find a reason to enter, even when the market is not offering a high-quality setup. A cleaner chart helps you wait. It makes it easier to distinguish between a real opportunity and a brief fluctuation that happens to satisfy one indicator while violating the broader structure. For many traders, that restraint is the difference between a method that looks sophisticated and a method that can actually be executed consistently.

The simplest test of any chart setup is whether it can be used the same way after a losing trade, a winning trade, or a week of mixed results. If the answer changes every time because you are constantly adding, removing, or reinterpreting indicators, the setup is too fragile. A repeatable process should let you scan a chart, identify the same conditions, and make the same type of decision without needing to renegotiate the rules. That does not mean the chart must be bare. It means every element on it should earn its place by improving clarity, not by increasing complexity.

CHAPTER 5

Chapter 5: Fundamental Analysis for Forex Traders

Fundamental analysis gives forex traders a way to interpret why a currency may be gaining or losing value beyond what the chart shows at any single moment. Instead of treating price as an isolated pattern, this approach places it inside a broader economic and policy context, where expectations about growth, inflation, labor conditions, and central bank action can shape demand for a currency over time. That context matters because forex prices often move not only on what has happened, but on how new information changes the market's view of what is likely to happen next.

Interest rates, inflation, employment data, and GDP as currency drivers

In forex, the most important fundamental drivers are often not the headline numbers themselves, but what those numbers imply about future policy, growth, and capital flows. Interest rates usually sit at the center of that process because they influence the return available on holding a currency. When a central bank raises rates, it can make that currency more attractive relative to others, especially if markets believe the tightening cycle will continue. But the reaction is rarely mechanical. Traders are not only comparing current yields; they are also pricing in the path of future rates, the credibility of the central bank, and whether the move was already expected. A rate hike that matches market expectations may produce little reaction, while a smaller-than-expected increase can trigger a sharp selloff if it signals a weaker policy stance than traders had assumed.

This is why the market often responds more strongly to expectations than to the release itself. A currency can rise before a central bank meeting if traders believe higher rates are coming, then fall after the decision if the bank sounds less aggressive than expected. The same logic applies in reverse. If a central bank appears willing to keep rates high for longer, the currency may strengthen even without a new hike. For traders, the practical point is that interest rates matter through the lens of relative policy. A currency does not need the highest nominal rate in the world to attract demand, but it does need a policy outlook that compares favorably with alternatives. That relative advantage becomes especially important in pairs where one central bank is tightening and the other is easing or signaling patience.

Inflation is the other major input into that policy outlook. Central banks watch inflation because persistent price pressure can force them to tighten policy, while weak inflation can give them room to cut rates or remain accommodative. For traders, inflation data matters not only because it affects the currency directly, but because it changes the expected central bank response. A hotter-than-expected consumer price reading can lift a currency if traders believe it increases the odds of higher rates. A softer reading can weaken it if it reduces the case for tightening. In that sense, inflation is often a currency driver through the policy reaction function rather than through the number alone. The market is asking: does this print change what the central bank is likely to do next?

Employment data works in a similar way, but with a broader signal about economic momentum. Strong labor-market conditions can support a currency because they suggest resilience in household income, consumption, and overall economic activity. Weak employment data can do the opposite, especially if it points to slowing growth and a greater chance of policy easing. In the United States, traders often focus on payrolls, unemployment, and wage growth because those figures can shift expectations for Federal Reserve policy quickly. But the same principle applies across economies: labor data is valuable because it helps the market judge whether growth is strengthening or fading. A single report may not change the trend, but a sequence of strong or weak releases can reshape the market's view of the currency's outlook.

GDP is the broadest of the four drivers, but it is not always the most tradable in the short term. Gross domestic product summarizes overall economic output, so it can confirm whether an economy is expanding or slowing, yet it often arrives with a lag and may already be partly priced in by the time it is released. Still, GDP matters because it anchors the larger narrative. If growth is accelerating, a currency may benefit from expectations of stronger capital inflows, firmer business activity, and a more supportive policy stance. If growth is deteriorating, the opposite can happen. Traders should also remember that GDP surprises can matter more when they conflict with the existing story. A country expected to slow may see its currency rally if GDP comes in far better than forecast, because the report forces a reassessment of policy and growth assumptions.

The real task is to connect these indicators instead of viewing them in isolation. A strong employment report, rising inflation, and resilient GDP can point in the same direction and create a more durable currency trend. But mixed signals can produce choppy price action. For example, inflation may be high enough to keep rates elevated, while GDP slows enough to raise recession concerns. In that kind of environment, the market may struggle to decide whether the currency should trade on policy support or growth weakness. That uncertainty often shows up as wider intraday swings, false breakouts, and faster reversals around news releases. Traders who understand the tension between growth and inflation are better prepared to avoid overreacting to one number when the broader macro picture is still unresolved.

It is also important to distinguish between a data surprise and a data trend. One report can trigger a sharp move, but sustained currency strength usually depends on repeated evidence that the economic picture is changing. Markets tend to care most when a pattern develops: inflation stays sticky, employment remains firm, or GDP consistently beats expectations. That pattern can shift the tone of central bank communication and alter positioning across the market. Research on macroeconomic news and financial markets has shown that scheduled announcements can produce measurable effects, especially when the information changes expectations rather than simply confirming them [113]. For the forex trader, that means preparation should focus not only on the calendar, but on the market's current assumptions going into the release.

In practice, these drivers are most useful when they help you frame the likely reaction, not predict the exact outcome. Before a major release, ask what the market is already expecting, which side of the policy debate the data will influence, and whether the event supports continuation or reversal in the current trend. A currency with favorable rate expectations may still fall if inflation or growth data weakens the case for future tightening. A currency under pressure may bounce if the report suggests the central bank has less reason to cut. The trader's advantage comes from reading the relationship between data, expectations, and policy rather than treating each release as a standalone event. That is where fundamental analysis becomes actionable: not in knowing the number after it prints, but in understanding what that number changes about the next move in the market.

Central bank policy, speeches, and market expectations

Central bank policy is one of the few forces in forex that can change the market's directional bias, volatility profile, and rate expectations at the same time. Traders often focus on the headline decision—whether a central bank raised, cut, or left rates unchanged—but the larger issue is how the decision alters the market's view of the future. A currency can rally even when a bank cuts rates if the cut was smaller than expected or if the statement signals that the easing cycle is ending. In other words, price is usually reacting to the gap between what was expected and what was delivered, not simply to the policy action itself.

This is why the policy statement, press conference, and supporting data often matter more than the rate move alone. Central banks communicate through multiple channels: the formal decision, the wording of the statement, the tone of the chair or governor, and the projections or guidance that follow. Traders listen for changes in language because those changes can reveal whether policymakers are becoming more concerned about inflation, growth, labor conditions, or financial stability. Even small wording shifts can matter if they change the market's assumption about how long rates may stay restrictive or how soon easing might begin. The market is constantly pricing the next move, and then the move after that.

Speeches are especially important because they can refine, reinforce, or sometimes contradict the most recent policy message. A central bank official may use a speech to emphasize that inflation remains above target, that policy is still data dependent, or that the committee is not committed to a preset path. Traders should treat these remarks as market inputs rather than as isolated commentary. The question is not whether a speech sounds aggressive or cautious in a general sense, but whether it changes the probability distribution the market has already built into price. That is why a single sentence about "higher for longer" can move yields, equities, and currencies if it forces participants to reprice the policy path.

Market expectations are the bridge between policy and price. By the time a central bank meeting arrives, the market has usually spent days or weeks forming a consensus view through economic data, analyst forecasts, futures pricing, and positioning. If the actual decision matches expectations, the immediate reaction may be muted even if the announcement sounds important on paper. If the decision surprises, the reaction can be sharp, but the direction still depends on whether the surprise is more hawkish or more dovish than the market had priced. This is one reason forex traders should pay attention to how much of a policy move is already "in the market" before the event. A widely anticipated hike can produce a selloff in the currency if the statement sounds less aggressive than expected.

For practical trading, the most useful habit is to separate the event into three layers: what the market expected, what the central bank actually did, and how the message changed future expectations. That framework helps prevent the common mistake of trading the headline alone. A rate decision that appears bullish for a currency may still fail if the press conference suggests policymakers are worried about growth or if forward guidance implies fewer hikes ahead. Likewise, a neutral decision can be supportive if the bank signals that inflation remains stubborn and policy will stay tight for longer than traders assumed. The move that matters is not always the obvious one.

Because central bank communication can reprice the entire front end of the yield curve, these events often create fast, uneven volatility. Electronic markets allow information to be absorbed almost immediately across participants and venues [14][15], which means spreads can widen, liquidity can thin, and price can jump through levels that would normally hold. That is especially important around scheduled announcements, when algorithms and discretionary traders are all responding to the same release within seconds. Studies of modern market structure also show that automated systems can intensify short-term movement and amplify market reactions when information arrives in concentrated bursts [101] [19]. For the forex trader, that means execution quality matters as much as direction. A correct view can still become a poor trade if it is entered into a thin, unstable market.

It is also important to remember that central bank policy does not operate in a vacuum. Inflation, labor conditions, growth concerns, and broader global stress all shape the policy path, and in periods of elevated uncertainty those trade-offs become more difficult to interpret. Recent research on inflation and macroeconomic strain highlights how policy decisions are often made in an environment where growth and price stability are pulling in different directions [26]. For traders, that means the same central bank can sound hawkish one month and cautious the next, not because it has become inconsistent, but because the underlying economic balance has changed. The best response is to track the evolving narrative, not just the last headline.

When you approach a policy event, the goal is not to predict every phrase a central banker will use. The goal is to understand what the market already believes, what would count as a surprise, and which currencies are most exposed to a shift in expectations. That kind of preparation helps you judge whether the event is likely to confirm the current trend, trigger a repricing, or produce a brief but tradable dislocation. In forex, central bank communication is not background noise. It is one of the clearest ways the market learns what future interest-rate conditions may look like, and that expectation often becomes the real driver of price.

News events, surprise releases, and volatility management

Scheduled economic releases are only one part of the event landscape. In practice, forex traders have to distinguish between expected risk and unexpected risk. Expected risk includes items already on the calendar: inflation reports, employment data, GDP, retail sales, central bank statements, and speeches. These events matter because the market often begins repricing before the number is published. The chart may look calm, but price can already be stretched around a consensus view, leaving the real move to occur only if the result differs enough from expectations. Unexpected risk is different. It comes from surprise headlines, geopolitical developments, policy leaks, emergency interventions, or sudden changes in market sentiment that are not fully reflected in advance. Research on news dissemination and financial markets supports the idea that textual information and surprise content can move prices sharply, especially when it changes how traders interpret future conditions [117][68].

That distinction changes how a trader should think about the calendar. The question is not simply whether an event is "important," but whether the market has had time to position for it and whether the release is likely to create a mismatch between expectation and reality. A central bank decision, for example, may be widely anticipated, yet the statement language, press conference tone, or forward guidance can still produce a large reaction because traders are not reacting only to the rate decision itself. High-frequency studies of monetary policy announcements show that exchange rates can become more volatile even when the headline rate does not change, which is a reminder that the market is often responding to the policy signal rather than the number alone [115]. For the trader, that means the release is not just a data point; it is a repricing event.

Surprise releases are especially dangerous because they can invalidate the assumptions behind a setup in seconds. A technically clean trade can fail not because the chart was wrong, but because the information environment changed faster than the structure could adapt. If price is already near a breakout level and a surprise release hits, the move may be amplified by trapped orders, widened spreads, and thin resting liquidity. The result can be a fast expansion that is difficult to enter cleanly and even harder to manage. This is one reason event-driven volatility often spills across related currency pairs rather than staying isolated in a single chart [119]. When one major currency re-prices, correlated pairs can react in ways that are not obvious from the original setup.

Volatility management begins before the event, not after it starts. A trader needs a rule for whether to participate, reduce risk, or stand aside. If the strategy depends on tight stops, precise entries, or normal spread conditions, then holding positions into a major release can turn a manageable loss into a distorted one. Spreads can widen, slippage can increase, and stop orders may fill at worse prices than expected. That does not mean every event must be avoided. It means the position size, stop placement, and trade objective have to match the environment. A small, preplanned exposure can be reasonable when the setup is based on a larger thesis and the trader is willing to absorb noise. A full-size trade with no event buffer is usually a different proposition.

One practical way to handle this is to separate trades into before-event, during-event, and after-event categories. Before-event trading is about positioning ahead of a release when the market may be underpricing a likely outcome. That approach requires strong conviction, wide enough risk parameters, and an acceptance that the first reaction may be erratic. During-event trading is the most difficult and is often best left to very experienced traders because execution quality can deteriorate quickly. After-event trading is usually the most accessible for developing traders, because it allows the market to reveal its initial interpretation first. In that case, the trader is not trying to predict the number; the trader is waiting for the market to show whether the surprise has been absorbed, rejected, or extended.

Even after the initial spike, the market may not settle immediately. Some releases create a one-way trend, while others produce a sharp first move followed by reversal as liquidity returns and traders reassess the implications. That is why the first candle after a headline is rarely enough information on its own. The better question is whether the move has follow-through, whether the market is holding above or below the release level, and whether the reaction is consistent with the broader fundamental backdrop. In research on exchange-rate modeling and forecasting, one recurring challenge is that the market is driven by changing expectations rather than static inputs [70]. A surprise matters most when it changes the path traders believe is likely from here, not merely when it prints a large deviation from the forecast.

For day-to-day trade management, the safest response to event risk is to make it explicit in the plan. That means checking the calendar before entry, knowing which releases affect the currencies being traded, and deciding in advance whether positions will be closed, reduced, or protected. It also means recognizing that not all volatility is equal. Some volatility is orderly and tradable; some is chaotic and expensive. The goal is not to avoid every fast market, but to avoid being forced into decisions when the market is least forgiving. If a release can change the trade thesis, then the thesis should be reviewed before the release, not during the spike. If it cannot change the thesis, then the position should be sized so that the event is a known risk rather than an open-ended threat.

Combining fundamental context with technical setups

Fundamental context becomes especially useful when it helps a trader decide which technical setups deserve attention and when they are likely to matter most. A chart pattern does not exist in isolation. A breakout in a currency pair tied to rising rate expectations is not the same as the same pattern forming in a pair facing a neutral policy outlook or a market already priced for disappointment. The technical structure may look identical, but the forces behind it are not. That difference is what keeps a trader from treating every setup as interchangeable.

The first step is to separate the broad fundamental backdrop from the immediate catalyst. Broad context includes the direction of monetary policy, relative growth trends, inflation pressure, and the market's current bias toward risk or caution. Immediate catalysts include scheduled data releases, central bank speeches, and surprise headlines that can accelerate or invalidate a setup. A trader does not need to forecast every macro outcome to use this information well. The goal is more modest: identify whether the background environment supports continuation, warns of instability, or argues for patience. Technical analysis then becomes the tool for timing, not the tool for inventing the trade idea from scratch.

One practical way to combine the two is to begin with the currency that has the clearest fundamental tailwind or headwind, then look for a technical structure that agrees with that direction. If a central bank is signaling tighter policy while inflation remains sticky, price may be more likely to respect pullbacks in that currency than to sustain countertrend rallies. In that setting, a trader might prefer trend continuation patterns, shallow retracements, or breakouts from consolidation rather than fading strength too early. On the other hand, when a currency is trading into a major event with the market heavily positioned, the technical picture may be less about direction and more about identifying where liquidity is likely to sit, such as prior highs, lows, and obvious support or resistance zones.

This is where many traders make a useful but incomplete distinction between "fundamental" and "technical" trading. In practice, the best decisions often come from layering them. Fundamentals help answer whether the market has a reason to move; technicals help answer whether the market is actually moving in a tradable way. A strong macro theme can remain dormant for days, then suddenly express itself through a clean breakout, a failed retest, or a trend resumption after a brief pullback. Studies in financial forecasting and adaptive trading consistently point to the value of combining multiple information sources rather than relying on a single input, especially in environments where patterns evolve and market regimes shift [50][90][123].

That said, not every fundamental development should override a clean technical setup. Traders often make the mistake of forcing a macro view onto a chart that is not ready to cooperate. If price is consolidating tightly and volume is contracting, the market may be waiting for confirmation rather than expressing conviction. If a pair is already extended after a strong move, chasing it simply because the news is favorable can leave the trader buying late into exhaustion. The better approach is to let fundamentals define the bias and let price action define the entry quality. When the chart and the macro backdrop point in the same direction, conviction improves. When they conflict, the trader should usually reduce size, wait for more information, or stand aside.

Event timing matters because fundamentals do not influence price evenly across the week. A setup that looks attractive several hours before a major release can become poor risk if the event is likely to trigger a volatility spike or a gap-like reaction in a highly liquid pair. In those moments, the technical level still matters, but the trader must understand that the market may temporarily ignore it. A support level can hold for days and then fail in seconds if the release changes expectations sharply. That is why pre-event planning should include not only direction but also exposure management: whether the trade should be entered before the event, after the reaction, or not at all.

It is also helpful to think in terms of alignment rather than certainty. A trade does not need a perfect macro story to be valid, and a solid fundamental backdrop does not guarantee that price will behave cleanly. The point is to improve odds by stacking evidence. A currency pair making higher lows near a support zone while the economic backdrop supports that currency is more attractive than the same pattern appearing against deteriorating policy expectations. Likewise, a bearish technical reversal carries more weight when it appears after a shift in rate expectations, weaker data, or a change in central bank tone. In a market where automated systems and fast-reacting participants can process large amounts of information quickly [81], the trader's edge often comes from disciplined selection: choosing the setups where context, structure, and timing all point in the same direction.

CHAPTER 6

Chapter 6: Proven Forex Trading Strategies

At this stage, the focus shifts from reading the market to organizing a repeatable way of trading it. A chart can suggest opportunity, but a strategy is what turns that opportunity into a defined decision process with clear conditions, manageable risk, and a consistent way to evaluate results. The goal is not to find a method that works in every market environment, because no such method exists; it is to understand how different approaches behave under different conditions so you can match your execution to the structure in front of you.

Trend-following strategies for capturing sustained market moves

Trend-following in forex is built around a simple idea: when a currency pair is moving with sustained momentum, the trader's job is not to predict the exact top or bottom, but to participate in the move while it remains intact. That sounds straightforward, yet it requires discipline because trend trading is less about finding perfect entries and more about aligning with the market's path of least resistance. In practice, that means identifying whether price is making a series of higher highs and higher lows in an uptrend, or lower highs and lower lows in a downtrend, and then waiting for conditions that favor continuation rather than chasing every burst of movement.

The first filter is context. Trend-following works best when the broader market is already showing directional commitment, whether that comes from policy divergence, shifting rate expectations, or a persistent capital flow theme. Exchange rates are affected by output, employment, inflation, and international capital flows [8], so a trend often has a macro reason behind it even if the chart is the only thing a trader sees. When that underlying force is strong enough, pullbacks tend to be temporary pauses rather than full reversals. The practical task is to distinguish a real trend from a noisy market that is simply oscillating inside a range. A moving average slope, a sequence of higher swing lows, and clean reactions at prior breakout levels can all help confirm that the market is still advancing in the same direction.

One of the most reliable trend-following entries is the pullback entry. Instead of buying after a sudden breakout candle or selling after a sharp breakdown, the trader waits for price to retrace toward a dynamic support or resistance area, such as a rising moving average, a prior breakout zone, or a previous swing level. The pullback should be measured, not destructive. In an uptrend, for example, a temporary dip that stalls above the prior higher low and then begins to turn back up often offers a better reward-to-risk profile than entering after an extended vertical move. This approach reduces the chance of buying into short-term exhaustion and gives the trader a more logical place for a stop-loss, usually beyond the point where the trend structure would be damaged if reached.

Breakout continuation is another useful trend-following model, but it should be used selectively. A breakout is only worth trading if it occurs in the direction of an already established trend and is supported by visible expansion in momentum. The market often pauses, consolidates, and then resumes in the trend direction once weaker participants have been shaken out. That consolidation can act as a launch point if price breaks away with enough conviction. The mistake is treating every new high or low as a valid signal. In a strong trend, the best breakouts usually occur after a compression phase, not after an extended move that is already far from its average pace. The more stretched the market becomes, the more a trader should expect hesitation or a deeper retracement before continuation.

Risk management is what keeps trend-following from turning into blind hope. Trends can last far longer than many traders expect, but they can also reverse suddenly when the market's narrative changes. Because of that, stops should be placed where the trend thesis is invalidated, not at arbitrary distances that merely feel comfortable. In an uptrend, that may mean below the most recent swing low or below a structure level that, if broken, would show that buyers have lost control. Profit management can be handled in stages: a partial exit at a predefined multiple of risk, followed by a trailing stop that protects gains while allowing the trade room to develop. The goal is to avoid cutting winners too early while also avoiding the temptation to hold every position indefinitely in the hope that a trend will continue forever.

Time frame alignment improves trend trading by preventing the trader from taking entries that conflict with the larger picture. A pair may be trending on the four-hour chart, but if the daily chart is pressing into major resistance, the move may be nearing exhaustion. Likewise, a short-term pullback inside a strong daily trend can offer a favorable entry only if the lower time frame shows the pullback losing momentum and the higher time frame still supports the broader direction. This layered view helps the trader avoid the common error of mistaking a temporary countertrend bounce for a genuine trend change. It also helps with patience, because not every chart needs immediate action. Sometimes the best trade is waiting for the market to finish correcting before it proves that the trend is still alive.

Trend-following also benefits from understanding that the strongest moves are often tied to broader shifts in market positioning and capital allocation. Capital flow waves can produce sustained exchange rate trends when money moves persistently toward one currency and away from another [128]. In those conditions, the market can grind in one direction for longer than traders accustomed to mean reversion expect. That is why trend followers often stay focused on structure and behavior rather than trying to forecast the exact fundamental catalyst. If price continues to respect support in an uptrend or resistance in a downtrend, the market is telling you that the prevailing imbalance is still in force. The trader's role is to stay with that imbalance until the chart shows that it has meaningfully changed.

Because trend-following depends on persistence, it is especially important to avoid overcomplicating the method. A clean setup usually beats a crowded one. If the pair is trending, the pullback is controlled, the entry level is logical, and the stop defines the invalidation point, the trade already has the essential ingredients. Additional indicators should only be used if they clarify the structure rather than obscure it. In forex, where liquidity, session timing, and macro expectations can all influence how long a move lasts, the trader who keeps the method simple is often better positioned to recognize when a trend is still worth following and when it has already done enough.

Range trading strategies for sideways markets

Range trading works best when price is trapped between clearly defined boundaries and the market lacks enough momentum to sustain a directional move. In that environment, the trader is not trying to catch an extended trend; the objective is to buy near support, sell near resistance, and manage the trade around the assumption that the range will continue until proven otherwise. That shift in mindset matters. A sideways market rewards patience, precision, and restraint more than prediction. If the market is balanced, the trader's edge comes from recognizing where that balance is likely to hold and where it is likely to fail.

The first task is to identify a range that is real, not imagined. A valid range usually has multiple touches on both the upper and lower boundaries, with price repeatedly rejecting those areas rather than slicing through them. The boundaries do not need to be exact to the pip, but they should be visible enough that other traders are likely to notice them too. It is also important to distinguish a true range from a temporary pause inside a larger trend. If the higher time frame still shows strong directional pressure, what looks like a sideways market on the intraday chart may only be a consolidation before continuation. In that case, fading every boundary can be a mistake.

Once the range is established, entries are usually taken near the edges, not in the middle. The center of a range is where reward-to-risk tends to deteriorate, because price can move in either direction with little warning and no immediate edge. Near support, a trader may look for signs that selling pressure is weakening: smaller downside candles, failed pushes lower, or a rejection wick that suggests buyers are stepping in. Near resistance, the same logic applies in reverse. The setup is not simply that price has touched a level; it is that price behavior suggests the level is still being respected. In practice, many traders wait for confirmation from price action before entering, rather than guessing that a level will hold on the first test.

Stops in range trading should be placed where the trade idea is clearly invalidated, not where the trader feels most comfortable. For a long position near support, that usually means below the range floor by enough room to account for noise and spread. For a short position near resistance, the stop belongs above the ceiling. Placing stops too tightly inside the range invites unnecessary losses from routine fluctuations. At the same time, stops that are too wide reduce the quality of the setup because the trader is taking on too much risk for a move that may only travel back toward the middle of the range. The goal is to align stop placement with the structure of the market, not with arbitrary point distances.

Profit targets should also be tied to the range structure. In a sideways market, the most natural target is often the opposite boundary or a logical midpoint if the trader is scaling out. That keeps expectations realistic and prevents the common mistake of treating a range trade like a trend trade. If the market is not showing signs of expansion, there is no reason to expect an outsized move. A trader who consistently aims for the far side of the range while risking only a fraction of that distance can maintain favorable trade economics even if not every setup works. This is one reason range trading can be attractive in quiet conditions: the structure itself provides a built-in framework for defining risk and reward.

False breakouts are one of the biggest challenges in sideways markets. Price will often pierce a boundary, attract breakout traders, and then snap back into the range. That behavior is not random; it reflects the market's habit of testing liquidity beyond obvious levels before deciding whether there is enough commitment to continue. For the range trader, the key is not to react emotionally to every brief excursion outside the box. A clean breakout is usually supported by follow-through, not just a single candle closing beyond the edge. If price returns quickly and closes back inside the range, that failure can sometimes create an opportunity in the opposite direction, but only if the trader has a clear rule for how much confirmation is required.

Range trading also benefits from context. A range in a low-volatility session may behave very differently from one forming ahead of a major economic release or after a sharp trend has already exhausted itself. If the broader backdrop suggests a catalyst is approaching, the range may be temporary and vulnerable to expansion. That is why range trading should be paired with awareness of the calendar and the higher time frame. Studies of trading systems and machine-learning-assisted decision models continue to show that market behavior is highly dependent on regime and that no single approach works equally well in every environment [98][87][134]. For the discretionary trader, the lesson is the same: the edge is not in forcing a trade, but in recognizing when the market is actually offering a sideways structure worth trading.

Because ranges can persist for long periods and then break abruptly, position sizing should remain conservative. A trader may see several successful bounces in a row and become overconfident, but a range that has held repeatedly can still fail without warning. That is especially true when liquidity shifts or new information changes the market's valuation of the currency pair. Range trading therefore works best when each trade is treated as a controlled attempt within a defined structure, not as a bet that the market must continue behaving the same way. The trader's task is to exploit repetition while respecting the possibility that the repetition will end.

Breakout strategies and how to filter false breakouts

A breakout strategy is built around the idea that price often spends time compressing before it expands. The market may coil inside a range, triangle, flag, or narrow consolidation as buyers and sellers reach temporary balance. When that balance breaks, the resulting move can offer strong follow-through because trapped traders are forced to react and new participants join the move. The challenge is that not every move beyond a boundary is a true breakout. Many are only brief excursions that fade once liquidity is absorbed. For that reason, a breakout trader is not simply watching for price to cross a level; the trader is looking for evidence that the move has enough force and acceptance to continue.

The first filter is the quality of the level itself. Breakouts matter more when they occur from clearly defined support or resistance that has been tested more than once and respected by the market. A level that is obvious on the chart tends to attract more orders, which makes the eventual break more meaningful. By contrast, a vague line drawn through random intraday noise is easier for price to pierce without consequence. It also helps to ask whether the level aligns with a larger market structure point, such as a prior swing high, swing low, session high, session low, or a major time-frame boundary. When several forms of structure line up, the breakout has a better chance of attracting real participation rather than just momentary attention.

Confirmation is the next filter, and it should come from price behavior rather than from a desire to avoid missing the move. A strong breakout often shows a decisive close beyond the level, not just a wick that briefly extends through it. The candle or candles surrounding the break should reflect commitment: expanding range, directional bodies, and follow-through rather than hesitation. In many cases, the market will break a level, pull back to retest it, and then continue. That retest can be useful because it shows whether the former barrier is now acting as support or resistance. If price returns to the level and immediately rejects it, the breakout is more credible. If it slips back through with ease, the market may have been running stops rather than starting a new leg.

False breakouts are often easier to recognize when you pay attention to context. A breakout that occurs deep inside a broader range or directly into a nearby higher-time-frame barrier has less room to run. The same is true when the move happens during thin liquidity or just before a major news release, when price can spike on temporary order flow and then reverse sharply. A trader should also be cautious when the breakout develops after an extended move, because late-stage breaks can be exhaustion events rather than fresh continuation. One of the most practical questions is simple: if this level gives way, is there enough open space for price to travel before meeting the next obstacle? If the answer is no, the breakout may be technically valid but still a poor trade.

Volume and volatility can help separate real expansion from noise. In forex, where centralized volume is not available in spot trading, tick volume can still provide a useful clue about participation. A breakout accompanied by stronger activity and wider price expansion is generally more convincing than one that happens quietly. But volume alone is not enough. A spike in activity can also occur during a stop hunt, especially when price sweeps a well-known level and then reverses. This is where combining tools matters. Research on technical analysis has shown that the value of chart-based methods depends heavily on how signals are filtered and tested, not on treating any single pattern as universally reliable [135][54]. Breakouts should be approached the same way: as setups that require context, not as automatic entries.

Entry technique is another place where traders improve their odds. Chasing the first tick beyond a level usually means paying the highest price for the least confirmation. A more disciplined approach is to wait for either a close beyond the level or a retest that holds. That patience often reduces the number of false breakouts taken in the heat of the moment. The trade-off is that some strong moves will run without a retest, so the trader must decide in advance what kind of breakout is being traded. If the strategy is designed for aggressive momentum entries, then smaller stops and faster decision-making are part of the plan. If the strategy is designed for confirmation, then missing the first portion of the move is an acceptable cost in exchange for better selectivity.

False breakout filters should be written into the trading plan before the chart is live. For example, a trader might require a breakout candle to close beyond the level, a retest to hold, and higher-time-frame space to the next barrier. Another filter might be avoiding breakouts that occur immediately before high-impact data, or only taking them when the move aligns with the session's usual volatility pattern. These rules do not eliminate losing trades, but they reduce the number of low-quality attempts. That is important because breakout strategies tend to produce a mix of small losses and occasional strong winners. Their edge comes from staying involved when expansion is real while stepping aside when price is merely probing for liquidity. Algorithmic and hybrid trading research has repeatedly emphasized that disciplined rule design and filtering improve execution quality more than raw signal frequency [81][136][137]. In discretionary breakout trading, the same principle applies: the best filter is not the most complicated one, but the one that keeps you out of the obvious traps.

Risk management has to match the behavior of the setup. A breakout entry should have a clearly defined invalidation point, usually just beyond the level that was supposed to hold after the break. If the level is violated again, the trade idea is no longer valid. That stop placement makes sense because breakout trades are built on acceptance. Once acceptance fails, the premise fails with it. Profit targets can be set at the next structure zone, measured move projection, or a multiple of the initial risk, but the target should reflect the fact that breakout trades are momentum trades, not random bets on continued excitement. The trader's job is to distinguish expansion from deception, then risk only enough on each attempt to survive the inevitable rounds where the market briefly breaks out and then turns back.

Swing trading versus day trading: choosing the right approach

Swing trading and day trading both aim to exploit short-term price movement, but they differ in how long a position is held, how much market noise must be tolerated, and how much attention the trader must give the screen. Swing traders typically hold positions for several days to several weeks, looking to capture a larger portion of a move that develops across multiple sessions. Day traders open and close positions within the same trading day, trying to benefit from intraday volatility while avoiding overnight exposure. Neither approach is inherently superior. The better choice depends on your schedule, temperament, capital, and ability to make decisions consistently under pressure.

The clearest practical difference is time horizon. Swing trading gives a setup more room to develop, which can reduce the need for constant monitoring and may allow the trader to focus on higher-quality trades that align with broader market structure. It also means accepting overnight risk, because price can gap or react sharply to news while the position is unattended. Day trading removes that overnight uncertainty, but it demands faster execution, tighter focus, and a willingness to make decisions in a compressed time frame. In forex, where liquidity and volatility shift across sessions, that difference matters. A trader who cannot monitor the market throughout the day may find day trading unrealistic, while a trader who dislikes overnight uncertainty may find swing trading uncomfortable.

Risk management also changes with the style. Swing trades generally require wider stops because they are designed to survive normal fluctuations over several sessions. That wider stop often means smaller position size if the trader is keeping risk per trade constant. Day trades usually use tighter stops and smaller targets, but the trade-off is that price noise can stop out a position before the intended move has time to unfold. Because of that, day trading can produce more frequent decisions and more frequent transaction costs, including spreads and slippage. A strategy with a modest edge can be weakened if the trader overtrades or pays too much in execution friction. Research on technical trading and intraday systems has long shown that the practical design of the strategy matters as much as the signal itself [54][140].

The right style should also match the market conditions you actually trade. Swing trading tends to work best when the market is building a directional move, reacting to macro themes, or moving in a way that develops over time rather than in a single burst. That makes it useful for traders who combine price action with fundamental context and want to avoid reacting to every intraday fluctuation. Day trading is more suited to periods of active session overlap, news-driven volatility, or clearly defined intraday ranges where price repeatedly offers short-lived opportunities. In both cases, the trader is not trying to predict every tick. The goal is to identify conditions where the chosen style has a reasonable chance of producing favorable follow-through. Since forex prices can change rapidly in response to economic and political forces [98], style selection should be tied to the type of movement you expect to see, not just the chart pattern in front of you.

Psychology is another deciding factor. Swing trading requires patience and tolerance for uncertainty. Once a position is open, the trader has to let the market work without interfering too early, which can be difficult if you are prone to micromanaging trades. Day trading requires a different discipline: the ability to stay focused, follow rules quickly, and avoid impulsive entries made from boredom or frustration. It can also intensify emotional swings because the feedback loop is immediate. A trader who is easily rattled by fast price changes may do better with swing trading, while a trader who becomes impatient when waiting for multi-day setups may prefer intraday activity. In either case, the style should reduce emotional conflict rather than create it.

Capital and lifestyle constraints should not be ignored. Swing trading can be more compatible with a full-time job or a limited schedule because it does not require constant screen time. It can also be more forgiving for traders who prefer to analyze the market once or twice a day and then let the trade play out. Day trading, by contrast, is a time-intensive process. It often demands a fixed routine around the most active sessions, rapid order execution, and a strong ability to review the market in real time. That intensity can be useful for some traders, but it can also lead to fatigue and overtrading. High-frequency environments, in particular, can magnify execution problems and sudden dislocations [41][105][141], which is one reason day traders need especially strict operational discipline.

A practical way to choose between the two is to test your own behavior before committing capital. Ask which style lets you follow your rules more faithfully. Ask which one fits your attention span, your available hours, and your tolerance for open risk. Then build a small sample of trades for each method and compare not only the profit and loss, but also the quality of your decisions. A style that looks attractive on paper may be too demanding in real time. Another may produce fewer opportunities but better execution and less emotional strain. The best approach is the one you can repeat with discipline, because consistency is what turns a trading idea into a workable process.

Backtesting and forward testing strategies before live execution

Before risking real capital, a strategy should prove two things: that it has a plausible edge under historical conditions and that it can be executed with enough consistency to survive live market pressure. Backtesting and forward testing serve different roles in that process. Backtesting asks how the method would have behaved on past data if the rules had been followed exactly. Forward testing asks how those same rules behave in real time, with current prices, changing volatility, and the emotional friction that comes from seeing a position move tick by tick. Used together, they help separate a strategy that merely looks good on a chart from one that can actually be traded.

A proper backtest begins with clearly defined rules. The entry trigger, stop placement, profit target, time filter, and exit conditions must be specific enough that another trader could apply them without improvising. If the rules are vague, the test becomes a story instead of an evaluation. That is especially important in forex because market conditions are not stable from one period to the next. Exchange rates are shaped by nonstationary behavior, low signal-to-noise conditions, intraday seasonality, and abrupt shifts in regime [143]. A strategy that works in a trending, high-volatility environment may fail in a quiet range, and a method that performs well on one currency pair may behave differently on another because of spread, liquidity, and session structure. The point of backtesting is not to prove that a strategy is universally profitable; it is to identify where it has a measurable edge and where it breaks down.

The quality of the test matters as much as the result. A strategy that is tested on a tiny sample or on cherry-picked periods can appear stronger than it really is. Good testing should include enough trades to be meaningful, multiple market environments, and realistic assumptions about execution. That means accounting for spreads, commissions if applicable, slippage, and the fact that the exact entry price in live trading is rarely identical to the theoretical price on a chart. If those costs are ignored, the backtest will usually overstate performance. The same caution applies to optimization. It is easy to keep adjusting parameters until the historical curve looks impressive, but excessive tuning often produces a method that fits the past too neatly and loses its edge when conditions change. Research on algorithmic trading and backtest environments consistently emphasizes the importance of disciplined process design, realistic execution assumptions, and careful validation rather than simple curve fitting [18][146].

One of the most useful habits in backtesting is to record not only the final outcome of each trade, but also the context around it. Was the pair in a strong trend or a choppy range? Was the trade taken during London, New York, or a quieter session? Was the setup aligned with the higher time frame or fighting it? Did news risk distort the result? These details help reveal whether the strategy is genuinely robust or whether it depends on a narrow set of favorable conditions. If a method only performs when the market is already moving strongly in one direction, that is not necessarily a weakness, but it is a constraint that must be understood. A trader who knows the conditions of edge can choose when to deploy the strategy and when to stay out of the market.

Forward testing is the bridge between historical analysis and live execution. A demo account or very small live position size allows the trader to observe how the method behaves in real time without exposing the account to unnecessary damage. This stage is valuable because it tests more than market logic. It tests whether the trader can follow the plan under pressure, whether entries are taken on time, whether stops are respected, and whether the method still makes sense when the next trade is not immediately available. In practice, many strategies fail forward testing not because the idea is flawed, but because the execution is inconsistent. That is why forward testing should be treated as a diagnostic phase, not as a formality.

Live market behavior can reveal problems that historical data hides. A setup may look clean in hindsight but be difficult to execute because price moves too quickly, spreads widen during the intended entry window, or the stop has to be placed so far away that the risk-to-reward profile becomes unattractive. This is one reason adaptive and data-driven trading systems receive so much attention in current research [50][144][145]. Markets change, and the trader's process has to account for that change rather than assume a static environment. For the discretionary trader, the lesson is similar: if a strategy performs well in backtesting but becomes hard to execute consistently in forward testing, the issue may be practical feasibility rather than statistical edge. A method that cannot be repeated with discipline is not ready for serious capital.

It is also important to distinguish between validation and temptation. A few profitable forward trades do not prove that a strategy is ready for full-size trading, just as a few losses do not disqualify it. The goal is to build confidence through evidence, not excitement. A sensible approach is to test the method across enough trades to observe its behavior in different conditions, then compare the live results with the historical expectations. If the forward sample is materially worse than the backtest, the trader should ask whether the rules are being followed, whether the market environment has changed, or whether the original test contained hidden bias. If the forward sample is broadly consistent, the strategy may be ready for gradual scaling. That transition should still be conservative, because the real test of any forex method is not whether it can win in a short burst, but whether it can be executed repeatedly without drifting away from the rules that gave it an edge in the first place.

CHAPTER 7

Chapter 7: Smart Risk Management and Position Sizing

Risk management is where a trading idea becomes a controlled business decision instead of a hopeful bet. By this point, the trader should already understand how setups are found and why they matter; the next step is deciding how much capital to commit when a valid opportunity appears. That decision affects everything that follows, from emotional pressure to long-term account survival, because even a strong method can be damaged by inconsistent exposure or oversized positions. In practice, the best traders do not think first about how much they might make; they think about how much they are prepared to lose if the market does not cooperate.

Determining risk per trade and setting maximum account exposure

Risk per trade is the amount of account equity you are willing to lose if a single position reaches its stop-loss. That definition sounds simple, but it is one of the most important numbers in trading because it forces you to think in terms of survival rather than prediction. A trader who knows in advance that no trade will cost more than a small, predetermined slice of capital is much less likely to let one mistake become a damaging event. In practical terms, this is where position sizing begins: the size of the trade should be determined by the distance to the stop and the amount of money you are prepared to lose, not by how convincing the setup looks.

For most traders, the first decision is the percentage of equity to risk on any one trade. There is no universal figure that fits every account, but the principle is the same: the percentage should be small enough that a normal losing streak does not create emotional pressure or force you to abandon the plan. Many traders use a fixed fraction of equity so that risk scales with the account. If the account grows, the dollar amount at risk grows modestly; if the account shrinks, exposure automatically contracts. That built-in adjustment is useful because it prevents a trader from taking the same dollar risk after a drawdown that they could comfortably absorb when the account was larger. The goal is not to maximize excitement on each trade; it is to preserve enough capital and mental stability to keep executing the method consistently.

Maximum account exposure is related, but it is not the same thing as risk per trade. Risk per trade measures the potential loss on one position. Account exposure describes how much of the account is committed across all open positions at the same time, including the effect of correlated trades. A trader can risk only a small amount on each individual trade and still be dangerously exposed if several positions are tied to the same currency, the same economic theme, or the same market event. For example, being long multiple pairs that all depend on the same base currency can create a much larger effective bet than the position tickets suggest. In other words, the account can be overcommitted even when each trade appears modest on its own.

That is why a risk limit should be built at two levels. First, define the maximum loss allowed on a single setup. Second, define the maximum combined exposure allowed across the portfolio. The second limit keeps a series of related trades from stacking into one oversized macro view. This matters in forex because currencies are linked through relative value, not isolated assets. A move in one major currency can affect several pairs at once, and those relationships can intensify during news events or shifts in rate expectations. A trader who ignores that connection may believe they have diversified risk when they have actually concentrated it. Market structure research emphasizes how exchange rates transmit changes in output, inflation, and capital flows across the global system, which is exactly why exposure needs to be monitored at the portfolio level [8].

A useful way to think about maximum exposure is to set a ceiling on the total risk you are willing to have open at one time, then allocate that ceiling carefully. If your account allows only a limited amount of drawdown before your decision-making deteriorates, your open risk should stay well below that threshold. This creates room for normal volatility, slippage, and the fact that stops are not always filled at the exact intended price. It also gives you flexibility when several opportunities appear simultaneously. Instead of forcing every setup to full size, you can rank them and assign risk where the technical and fundamental case is strongest. That discipline reduces the temptation to treat every signal as equally important.

Exposure limits should also reflect the trader's style and the market environment. A short-term day trader may have several open positions during a session, but those positions still need to be treated as a single risk picture if they are all sensitive to the same economic release or intraday dollar move. A swing trader may hold fewer trades, yet those trades can remain vulnerable for days to changes in sentiment, central bank expectations, or broad risk appetite. The correct limit is not simply about how many trades are open; it is about how much damage the account can absorb if several positions move against you together. That is especially important when volatility rises, because correlated pairs can widen and reverse more sharply than they did during quieter conditions.

In practice, the discipline comes from reducing the decision to a repeatable calculation before the order is placed. Determine the account value, choose the maximum percentage you are willing to risk, measure the stop-loss distance in pips or points, and size the position so the dollar loss at the stop matches your limit. Then check whether the new trade would push total open exposure beyond your ceiling. If it would, reduce the size or pass on the setup. This process may feel restrictive at first, but it is the opposite: it protects the trader from emotional overcommitment and from the common mistake of letting a promising chart override basic capital preservation. A trading plan becomes far more reliable when the amount at risk is decided by rule rather than by impulse, especially in a market where competition, technology, and speed continue to raise the cost of undisciplined behavior [147].

Position sizing formulas and how leverage affects outcomes

Position sizing is the bridge between a trading idea and the actual dollar risk taken on the account. Two traders can enter the same pair at the same price with the same stop-loss and still produce very different outcomes because they sized the position differently. That is why the sizing formula matters as much as the setup itself: it determines how much of your account is exposed if the trade fails, and it keeps the loss aligned with your plan rather than with your emotions.

The most common framework is based on account risk and stop distance. First, decide how much of your account you are willing to lose on one trade. Then measure the distance between your entry and stop-loss in pips or points. Finally, translate that distance into the number of units or lots that keeps the loss within your limit. In simple terms, the formula is:

Position size = Account risk amount ÷ Trade risk per unit

If you prefer to think in lot terms, the same logic applies. For example, if a $10,000 account risks 1% per trade, the maximum loss is $100. If the stop-loss on EUR/USD is 50 pips and each pip on a standard lot is worth about $10, then one standard lot would risk about $500, which is far above the limit. To stay near $100 of risk, the trader would need roughly one-fifth of a standard lot, or 0.20 lots, because 50 pips at that size would approximate the intended loss. The exact pip value depends on the pair, the account currency, and the lot size, so the calculation should always be checked before the order is placed.

A useful way to think about this is to separate risk from exposure. Risk is the amount you can lose if the stop is hit. Exposure is the notional size of the position, which is often much larger than the risk amount because the stop defines the loss boundary. This distinction is especially important in forex, where leverage can make a small margin deposit control a much larger position. A trader may only need a fraction of the position value as margin, but that does not reduce the amount at risk if price moves against the trade.

Leverage amplifies outcomes by increasing the size of the position you can control relative to your account equity. Used carefully, it allows efficient capital use and makes smaller accounts more practical for trading. Used carelessly, it magnifies the speed at which losses accumulate. The key point is that leverage does not change the math of the stop-loss; it changes how large the position can be relative to the account. A 20-pip loss on a modestly sized position may be manageable, while the same 20-pip move on an oversized leveraged position can create serious damage.

This is why high leverage should never be confused with high risk tolerance. A broker may offer 50:1, 100:1, or even more, but that is only the ceiling on what can be controlled, not a recommendation for what should be used. In practical trading, the question is not, “How much leverage is available?" but "How much of that leverage is necessary to express the trade while keeping risk inside the plan?" The safest answer is usually the smallest position that still allows the setup to be traded with consistency. Research on automated and quantitative trading methods continues to show that execution logic and discipline matter greatly in fast-moving, nonlinear markets [98][83][77][131].

Consider two traders with the same $10,000 account and the same 1% risk limit. Trader A uses a 40-pip stop and sizes the trade properly so the maximum loss is $100. Trader B uses the same stop but doubles the position size because the margin requirement looks small. If price reaches the stop, Trader A loses 1% of the account; Trader B loses 2%. That difference may seem minor on one trade, but over a series of losses it compounds quickly. A string of five losing trades would put Trader A down about 5%, while Trader B would be down about 10%, which is a much harder hole to recover from.

Leverage also affects psychology. When a position is too large, every tick feels meaningful, and that pressure often leads to premature exits, moving stops, or abandoning the plan. When a position is sized correctly, the trader can let the stop do its job without needing to interfere. That calm is not a luxury; it is part of the edge. The purpose of leverage is not to maximize excitement or chase oversized gains. Its purpose is to make the position efficient while preserving the trader's ability to think clearly and execute the plan consistently.

In practice, position sizing should be recalculated every time the stop distance changes. A wider stop requires a smaller position; a tighter stop allows a larger one, but only if the stop is placed for valid market reasons and not simply to justify more size. If the trade idea requires a stop that is too wide for the chosen risk limit, the correct response is usually to reduce size or skip the trade, not to stretch the account's tolerance. That discipline keeps leverage working as a tool rather than turning it into a hidden source of account volatility.

Stop-loss placement, take-profit planning, and risk-to-reward ratios

Stop-loss placement begins with a simple idea: the trade must have a clearly defined point where the original setup is proven wrong. That point should not be chosen because it feels comfortable or because it preserves a round number of pips. It should be chosen because, if price reaches that area, the reason for entering no longer holds. In other words, the stop belongs to the market structure, not to the trader's preference. If a long trade is based on a breakout above resistance, the stop usually belongs somewhere that invalidates the breakout, not just a few pips below the entry. If a short trade is based on a failed rally, the stop should sit beyond the area where sellers were expected to defend. When stops are placed too close, normal noise can remove the position before the move develops. When they are placed too far away, the trade may still be valid, but the risk may become too large to justify the setup.

Good stop placement also requires attention to volatility and to the behavior of the specific pair being traded. A stop that makes sense on EUR/USD during a quiet session may be far too tight on a more volatile pair or during a major news release. The market does not move in a uniform way, and the same distance from entry can mean very different things depending on session conditions, average daily range, and recent price expansion. Traders often make the mistake of using the same fixed stop distance for every setup. A better approach is to ask whether the stop is wide enough to survive ordinary fluctuation but tight enough to protect the account if the market is genuinely moving against the idea. That balance is especially important because stop-loss orders can contribute to rapid price movement when many are clustered around the same area [152].

Placement should also reflect the chart level that actually matters. If price has repeatedly respected a swing low, that low may be a logical place to define risk on a long trade. If a range boundary has held several times, the stop should not sit directly on that boundary where a brief probe can trigger it. Likewise, if the setup depends on a moving average, a trendline, or a prior consolidation zone, the stop should be positioned beyond the point where that support would no longer be meaningful. The goal is not to hide the stop where it is least likely to be hit; the goal is to place it where the market has enough room to behave normally while still telling you, with clarity, that the trade is no longer working.

Take-profit planning should be built with the same discipline. A target is not just the place where a trader hopes to get paid; it is the point where the market is likely to encounter opposition, slow down, or complete the expected move. That means profit targets should be tied to structure as well: prior highs and lows, measured move projections, range boundaries, or major support and resistance zones. A trade that has room to run should not be cut short simply because a fixed pip target was chosen in advance without reference to the chart. At the same time, a target that sits too far beyond realistic market structure can turn a good trade into a frustrating one, especially if the pair is more likely to stall before reaching it. Planning the exit in advance helps remove the temptation to improvise once the trade is live.

There is also a difference between a target that is technically possible and one that is statistically sensible. Many traders focus on how much they want to make rather than on how much the market is likely to offer under the current conditions. A target should be large enough to justify the risk, but it should also be reachable often enough to support the strategy over time. That is why take-profit planning works best when it is based on repeated market behavior rather than on wishful thinking. In some cases, the first logical target may be near enough to secure partial profit or reduce exposure, while the remainder of the position is left open for a larger move. In other cases, the best choice is to take the full position off at the first major objective and wait for a new setup rather than forcing the trade to do more than the market is likely to allow.

This is where the risk-to-reward ratio becomes a practical decision tool rather than a slogan. The ratio compares the amount at risk to the amount expected to be gained if the target is reached. If a trade risks 30 pips to pursue 60 pips, the ratio is 1:2. If it risks 25 pips to pursue 75 pips, the ratio is 1:3. On the surface, higher ratios look better, but the number alone does not determine quality. A trade with a very high target may have a lower probability of reaching it, while a trade with a modest target may be reached more consistently. The useful question is whether the setup offers enough reward relative to the defined risk to make the trade worth taking across a series of attempts. A strategy can be profitable with a moderate win rate if the average winner is meaningfully larger than the average loser.

The ratio should be judged alongside execution quality and trade frequency. A setup that offers 1:4 on paper is not necessarily superior if it requires a stop so wide that position size becomes too small to matter, or if the target is so ambitious that the trade rarely gets there. Likewise, a 1:1.5 trade may be acceptable if the pattern is highly reliable and the market conditions favor quick follow-through. The point is not to chase the biggest theoretical number, but to ensure that the trade has a logical edge before capital is committed. Because clustered stops can fuel sharper moves once triggered, especially in fast markets [152], traders should avoid placing stops and targets in obvious, crowded locations when they can be refined by structure and context.

In practice, the best trade plans define all three elements together: where the setup fails, where the market is likely to respond, and whether the reward justifies the exposure. If any one of those parts is vague, the whole trade becomes harder to manage. A trader who knows the stop, the target, and the expected ratio before entry is not trying to predict every tick; the trader is simply making sure the position has a logical boundary on both sides. That discipline does not guarantee a winning trade, but it does prevent a losing trade from becoming undefined, and in forex that distinction matters as much as the entry itself.

Managing correlated pairs, drawdowns, and portfolio-level risk

Correlated pairs can make a portfolio look diversified when it is not. In forex, many pairs share the same underlying currency, the same macro driver, or the same risk sentiment, so taking several positions at once can quietly multiply exposure to a single idea. A trader long EUR/USD, GBP/USD, and AUD/USD, for example, is not holding three independent bets if the U.S. dollar weakens broadly; that is one theme expressed through three instruments. The chart may show three separate setups, but the account is carrying a concentrated view on the dollar. Managing that concentration starts with recognizing that correlation is not a fixed number. It changes as central bank expectations shift, as risk appetite expands or contracts, and as markets move from calm conditions into stress.

A practical way to think about correlation is to ask what each trade is really expressing. A long position in EUR/USD and a short position in USD/CHF both benefit from dollar weakness, even though the pairs look different on the screen. Likewise, AUD/USD and NZD/USD often respond to similar growth and commodity themes, while EUR/GBP can behave differently because it is driven more by relative policy expectations between two European economies. When positions are built from the same currency theme, risk should be sized as if the trader has one larger trade rather than several smaller ones. That does not mean avoiding all related pairs. It means understanding that adding a second or third correlated position increases the probability that one macro move will hit the whole basket at once.

This matters most when volatility rises. During quiet conditions, correlated pairs may drift together without creating much immediate harm. But in a fast market, correlations often tighten, and losses can stack quickly. A central bank surprise, a major inflation release, or a sharp shift in global risk sentiment can cause several pairs to move in the same direction within minutes. That is why portfolio-level risk should be measured in aggregate, not trade by trade. If each position risks 1 percent of equity, three highly correlated positions can create a much larger effective exposure than 3 percent, because the same event can trigger all three stops. The trader's first defense is to cap the amount of capital exposed to one currency or one market theme, not just to one setup.

Drawdown management is the next layer of control. A drawdown is not simply a losing streak; it is the decline from a prior equity peak, and it becomes dangerous when it changes behavior. Many traders can follow their plan when the account is near highs, then begin to improvise once equity falls. They widen stops, increase size to recover faster, or abandon valid filters because the pressure to "make it back" becomes stronger than the discipline to protect capital. A drawdown plan should be written before it is needed. That plan can include a maximum percentage decline at which trading size is reduced, a deeper threshold at which trading stops for review, and a rule that prevents immediate retaliation after a loss. The purpose is not punishment. It is to stop a temporary slump from turning into a structural account problem.

One useful habit is to separate normal variance from damage. Even a sound strategy will experience losing runs, and a trader who expects equity to rise in a straight line will misread ordinary fluctuation as failure. The question is whether the drawdown is still within the range that the method historically produced. If the answer is yes, the response should usually be restraint and adherence to plan, not a complete overhaul. If the answer is no, then the issue may be execution, market regime, or position sizing. In that case, the trader should reduce risk before continuing. Research on adaptive and automated trading systems in changing market conditions reinforces a principle that applies just as well to discretionary trading: methods can degrade when the environment changes, so risk controls must be able to respond [82][58][89].

At the portfolio level, the goal is not only to limit loss, but to prevent hidden overlap. That means grouping trades by currency, by macro driver, and by volatility regime. A basket of dollar-sensitive longs is one group. Several commodity-linked currencies are another. Positions taken ahead of the same event, such as a central bank meeting or inflation release, also belong in the same risk bucket even if they are on different pairs. Some traders use a simple exposure cap per currency, such as limiting total risk tied to any single currency to a small fraction of the account. Others track a "theme budget," where all trades built on the same thesis share one combined ceiling. The exact number matters less than the discipline of applying the same rule every time.

Portfolio risk also includes the interaction between position management and market structure. A cluster of small losses can be acceptable if each trade was independent and sized correctly. What is far more dangerous is a sequence of losses that all come from the same mistaken assumption. Studies of market microstructure and position management show that individual trading decisions can shape future price formation, but they also emphasize that traders are influenced by recent market information and by their own prior actions [155]. In practice, that means a trader who has been stopped out several times on related pairs should not simply re-enter because the chart still looks familiar. The portfolio may be telling a different story than the single chart. When several positions begin to move together, the account itself becomes the chart that matters most.

For that reason, the best portfolio control is often a combination of simple rules: limit total correlated exposure, reduce size during elevated volatility, define a maximum drawdown threshold, and review all open positions as a set rather than as isolated trades. This is especially important when using leverage, because leverage magnifies not only individual losses but also the effect of correlation across the whole account. A trader who keeps each trade small but ignores overlap can still suffer a large portfolio loss if the market reprices one currency theme across multiple pairs at once. Managing correlated pairs, drawdowns, and portfolio-level risk is therefore less about prediction than about making sure no single market move can dictate the fate of the account.

CHAPTER 8

Chapter 8: Trade Execution and Order Management

Once a trade idea has been validated, the quality of the execution becomes the next test of discipline. A sound setup can still underperform if the order is placed carelessly, the entry is rushed, or the trade is managed without a clear plan for what happens after it is live. In modern markets, where electronic trading has made participation faster and more continuous [21][15], execution is not a mechanical afterthought but part of the strategy itself. The trader must know in advance how the order will be entered, how the position will be monitored, and what conditions justify an adjustment rather than a reaction.

Market orders, limit orders, stop orders, and when to use each

Order type determines how your instruction interacts with the market, and that interaction matters as much as the trade idea itself. A market order tells the broker to execute immediately at the best available price. A limit order tells the broker to wait for a specific price or better. A stop order tells the broker to activate once price reaches a trigger level, usually to enter a trade in the direction of momentum or to protect an existing position with an exit. In forex, where prices can move quickly and spreads can widen, the difference between these instructions is not academic. It affects entry quality, fill certainty, and the amount of slippage a trader may experience.

A market order is the simplest tool and the one most often used when speed matters more than precision. If price is moving into a breakout, or if a news-driven move is already underway and the trader needs immediate participation, a market order ensures the trade is filled without waiting. That can be useful when the setup has already been confirmed and missing the move would be more costly than accepting a slightly less favorable entry. The tradeoff is that the fill may not match the quote visible a moment earlier. In fast markets, the difference between the expected price and the executed price can be meaningful, especially around major releases or during thin liquidity periods.

Limit orders serve the opposite purpose. They are designed for patience and price control. A buy limit is placed below the current market, and a sell limit is placed above it, each at a level where the trader wants to be filled only if price improves to that point. This makes limit orders useful for pullback entries, range trading, and situations where the trader has identified a preferred price zone and is willing to wait for it. The advantage is precision: if the market reaches the level, the fill is generally no worse than the limit price. The risk is nonexecution. A strong setup can move away without ever touching the limit, and a trader who insists on perfect price may repeatedly miss valid opportunities.

Stop orders are best understood as trigger orders. A buy stop sits above the current price and becomes active when price rises to that level; a sell stop sits below the current price and becomes active when price falls to that level. Traders use them in two distinct ways. First, they can be entry orders for breakout strategies, allowing participation only if price proves that it has moved beyond a key boundary. Second, they can be protective exit orders, commonly called stop-loss orders, that close a trade if price moves against the position. In both cases, the logic is the same: the market must travel to a specific point before the instruction is triggered. That makes stop orders valuable when the trader wants confirmation that momentum has actually reached a threshold, but they can also be vulnerable to brief spikes that trigger the order and then reverse.

The choice among these order types should be tied to the structure of the setup, not to habit. If the trade thesis depends on immediate participation, a market order may be appropriate. If the thesis depends on price returning to a measured area of value, a limit order is usually better. If the thesis depends on price proving that it has broken through resistance, support, or an intraday range boundary, a stop order may fit the logic of the trade. A trader who uses the wrong order type can undermine the setup before the position even has a chance to work. For example, entering a breakout with a limit order may leave the trader unfilled, while entering a pullback setup with a market order may sacrifice the favorable price that made the trade attractive in the first place.

Execution quality also depends on the market environment. During highly liquid sessions, market orders and stops often behave more predictably because there is enough depth to absorb activity. Around major news events, however, spreads can widen and liquidity can thin abruptly, which makes market and stop orders more exposed to slippage. Limit orders can avoid paying worse prices, but they may not fill at all if the market moves too quickly through the level. This is why order selection should be linked not only to the chart pattern but also to the time of day, the event calendar, and the pair being traded. A major pair during London or New York hours behaves differently from an exotic pair during a quiet session, and the order type should reflect that difference.

It is also important to distinguish between the order used to enter and the order used to manage risk. A trader may enter with a market order, for example, but still place a stop-loss as a protective stop order at the level where the setup is invalidated. Likewise, a breakout trade may be entered with a buy stop, while the protective stop-loss is placed below the breakout structure. Thinking clearly about this distinction helps prevent confusion and improves consistency. The entry order answers the question of how to get into the trade. The protective order answers the question of where the trade is proven wrong. When those two decisions are made separately and deliberately, execution becomes part of the strategy rather than a last-second reaction to price.

Planning entries and exits before placing a trade

A trade should be planned from the moment the idea is formed, not after the order is live. That means the entry, the exit, and the conditions that invalidate the setup should already be defined before any capital is committed. If those decisions are left open-ended, the trade becomes vulnerable to hesitation on the entry, emotional interference during the hold, and improvisation at the exit. Planning ahead removes ambiguity. It also forces the trader to think in terms of process rather than impulse, which is essential if the goal is consistency instead of occasional luck.

The entry should be tied to a specific market condition, not to a vague feeling that price "looks ready." In practice, that usually means waiting for a level, pattern, or trigger that confirms the setup is active. A breakout trader may require price to close beyond resistance and hold there long enough to show acceptance. A pullback trader may need a retracement into a defined zone before entering in the direction of the larger move. A range trader may want price to test support or resistance with enough evidence that the boundary is still being respected. The point is not to make entry perfect; it is to make it deliberate. A defined trigger prevents random participation and keeps the trader from chasing price after the move has already become extended.

Once the entry is defined, the exit plan should be built around both protection and objective. Protection comes first. Every trade needs a point where the idea is no longer valid, and that point should be identified before the order is placed. If the market reaches that level, the trade is wrong, or at least wrong enough that staying in no longer fits the original thesis. Objective is the other side of the equation: if the trade works, where will profits be taken, partially reduced, or protected? Some traders use a fixed target based on structure, such as the next support or resistance area. Others use a measured move, a volatility-based target, or a trailing method that allows the market to decide how far the move can extend. Whatever the method, the exit should be consistent with the strategy being traded. Studies comparing technical and fundamental approaches continue to show that neither works as a universal answer; the stronger edge comes from disciplined rules and execution, not from improvisation [86].

A useful way to think about the exit is to separate the trade into two questions: “Where am I wrong?” and “Where is the opportunity likely to end?” The first question defines the stop-loss. The second defines the take-profit. If those two points are too close together, the trade may be vulnerable to normal noise. If they are too far apart, the trade may require an unrealistic move to justify the risk. This is why planning entries and exits cannot be isolated from risk management. A trade with a beautiful chart pattern but a poor risk-to-reward profile is still a weak trade. The structure of the market should support the planned exit, not force it. In that sense, the exit plan is not a separate step after entry; it is part of the original analysis.

It also helps to predefine how the trade will be managed if price behaves in a mixed or uncertain way. Markets do not always move cleanly from entry to target. Price may stall, pull back, or test the entry area again before deciding. If those possibilities are not accounted for in advance, the trader is left making emotional decisions in real time. A plan might specify that no adjustment will be made unless price closes beyond a certain level, or that one portion of the position will be reduced at the first target while the rest is protected with a stop at break-even or beyond structure. The key is that the rules are known before the trade begins. That way, any adjustment is an execution of a plan rather than a reaction to discomfort.

Order placement should reflect the same discipline. A market order may be appropriate when speed matters more than precision, but a limit or stop order may better match a setup that depends on price reaching a specific level first. The trader should decide in advance whether the trade requires confirmation, whether a missed fill is acceptable, and whether slippage would materially damage the setup. This is especially important around fast-moving events or thin liquidity, where a good idea can turn into a poor execution if the order type is chosen carelessly. Research on trading-system development consistently emphasizes that the rules used to enter and exit a trade must be testable and repeatable, because a strategy cannot be evaluated honestly if the execution changes from trade to trade [3].

The simplest way to keep the plan intact is to write it down in concrete terms before the order is sent. A complete pre-trade plan should answer four questions: what must happen for the entry to be valid, where the stop belongs, where the first profit target sits, and what will be done if price stalls or extends farther than expected. When those answers are explicit, the trader can execute with less hesitation and fewer second guesses. That does not remove uncertainty from the market, but it does remove uncertainty from the decision-making process. In forex, where conditions can change quickly and false moves are common, that distinction is one of the most valuable forms of control a trader can have.

Managing trades in real time: scaling out, trailing stops, and adjustments

Once a trade is live, the question changes from should I be in this trade? to how do I manage what the market is now doing? That shift matters because a position is no longer a static idea after entry; it becomes a sequence of decisions under changing conditions. Good real-time management is not about reacting to every small fluctuation. It is about protecting the original edge while allowing the trade enough room to develop. In practice, that means deciding ahead of time which adjustments are allowed, which ones are forbidden, and what information justifies changing course.

Scaling out is one of the most practical tools for reducing pressure while still participating in a larger move. Instead of closing the entire position at one target, a trader may take partial profits as price reaches predefined milestones. This can make sense when the setup has room to extend but the market has already delivered a meaningful move. By banking part of the gain, the trader lowers open risk and removes some emotional strain from the decision-making process. The danger is scaling out too early or too often, which can leave the remaining position too small to matter. If every little push is used as an excuse to trim, the trade may become safe but unproductive. A better approach is to tie partial exits to structure: prior support or resistance, measured move objectives, major intraday levels, or a zone where momentum is likely to slow.

Trailing stops serve a different purpose. They are designed to protect open profit while giving the market room to continue in the trade's favor. A trailing stop should not be placed so tightly that normal volatility knocks it out before the move has a chance to mature. Nor should it be so loose that it fails to preserve much of anything. The best trailing method depends on the style of trade. Some traders trail behind swing highs and lows, moving the stop only when structure confirms continuation. Others use a volatility-based distance, such as a multiple of average range, to avoid getting clipped by ordinary noise. A trailing stop is most effective when it follows the market's behavior rather than the trader's hope. If price is making higher lows in a long trade, the stop can rise behind those lows. If momentum fades and structure weakens, the stop should reflect that change instead of remaining anchored to the original entry.

Adjustments during the life of a trade should be made with restraint. Many traders damage otherwise sound positions by moving stops farther away after entry, adding size without a plan, or changing the target every time price hesitates. Those actions usually come from discomfort, not analysis. A valid adjustment is one that responds to new information. For example, if price clears a key barrier with strong follow-through, it may justify reducing risk on the remainder of the position or trailing more aggressively. If a news release is approaching and the trade has already reached a logical profit zone, it may make sense to reduce exposure before the event. If the market is stalling in a narrow range after an impulsive move, the trader may decide that the original target is no longer realistic and take partial profit rather than waiting for a continuation that is not developing. The important point is that the adjustment should be based on market structure, volatility, or event risk —not on the urge to interfere.

Real-time management also requires awareness of time. A trade that is still technically valid can become less attractive if it takes too long to move. Capital tied up in a stagnant position has an opportunity cost, especially for active traders who can only monitor a limited number of setups. If a position has not progressed within the expected time window, that may signal weakness even if price has not violated the stop. Time-based rules can be useful here. A trader might decide that if a breakout does not continue within a certain number of candles, the trade will be reduced or exited. This is not about forcing every position to move quickly; it is about recognizing that a trade's edge often depends on how promptly the market confirms the idea.

Execution quality matters throughout the management process. Partial exits, stop adjustments, and re-entry decisions all interact with spread, slippage, and market speed. In fast conditions, especially around major releases or session opens, a stop order may fill worse than expected and a limit order may not fill at all. That is why management rules should be simple enough to execute under pressure. A trader who needs to make five discretionary choices in the middle of a volatile move is more likely to improvise badly. The cleaner method is to define the main branches in advance: where to take the first partial, when to tighten the stop, when to leave the trade alone, and when the setup is no longer valid. Real-time management becomes far more reliable when it is treated as the execution of a plan rather than a fresh round of judgment on every tick.

There is also a psychological benefit to structured trade management. Partial profits can reduce the temptation to micromanage, while a well-placed trailing stop can prevent a profitable trade from turning into a loss. At the same time, both tools can be misused if they are treated as emotional relief valves. The goal is not to eliminate discomfort; it is to keep discomfort from controlling the decision. A trader who knows in advance what will happen at each stage of the trade can sit through normal noise more calmly and avoid the common habit of changing the plan after the market has already started to test it. Over time, that discipline is what turns execution from a stressful reaction into a repeatable process.

Handling slippage, spreads, and execution quality

Slippage, spreads, and execution quality are not separate annoyances to deal with after the fact; they are part of the actual cost of trading. A setup that looks profitable on the chart can become mediocre once the spread is paid, and a trade that should have been exited at a defined price can end up a few pips worse if the market moves quickly. In a market where liquidity changes from one session to the next and large orders are absorbed gradually rather than all at once, price formation is not instantaneous [159]. That matters because the trader is not trading an abstract line on a screen. The trader is interacting with a live market that may fill orders at slightly different prices depending on urgency, volatility, and available liquidity.

Spread is the simplest of the three to understand, but it is often underestimated. The spread is the gap between the bid and ask, and it represents an immediate cost the trader must overcome before a position can move into profit. In highly liquid major pairs during active sessions, spreads are usually tighter and easier to absorb. In thinner conditions, around news releases, or in less liquid pairs, spreads can widen enough to change the economics of a trade. This is one reason a strategy that works on a backtest can disappoint in live trading if the test assumed unrealistically low transaction costs. A trader should always treat the spread as part of the entry price, not as a minor detail to be ignored. For short-term methods, especially those targeting small moves, the spread can consume a large share of the expected edge.

Slippage is different because it occurs when the execution price differs from the requested price. It can be negative, when the fill is worse than expected, or positive, when the fill is better. In fast markets, the gap between the decision and the fill can widen because price has moved before the order reaches the market or before the available liquidity at that level is consumed. This is especially important for market orders and for stop orders triggered during sharp volatility. A stop-loss is not a guarantee of a specific fill price; it is an instruction to exit when a level is reached, and in a fast move the actual exit may occur beyond that level. The practical lesson is that risk should be planned with a cushion. If a trade can only tolerate a very exact stop, it may be too fragile for real-market conditions.

Execution quality is the broader measure that ties these issues together. It includes whether the order was filled at a fair price, whether the fill was delayed, whether the broker's platform handled the order cleanly, and whether the trade experienced unnecessary friction from wide spreads or poor routing. Good execution quality does not mean every trade is filled at the ideal price. It means the market interaction is consistent with the trading plan and close enough to preserve the strategy's edge. In modern markets, where electronic systems and algorithmic participants dominate a large share of activity, execution speed and process discipline matter more than ever [18] [41]. That is true for retail traders as well, even if their order flow is smaller. A delayed or poorly handled order can turn a valid setup into a distorted result.

One of the most effective ways to manage these costs is to match order type to market conditions. Market orders are useful when immediate participation matters more than precision, but they expose the trader to slippage if the market is moving quickly. Limit orders control price better, though they may miss the trade entirely if price never returns to the desired level. Stop orders are often used to enter breakouts or protect open positions, but they are vulnerable to fast moves and temporary spikes. The right choice depends on the structure of the setup and the current liquidity environment. If the market is calm and the pair is liquid, execution tends to be cleaner. If the market is thin or event-driven, the trader should expect more friction and plan accordingly.

There are several practical habits that improve execution without adding unnecessary complexity. First, avoid trading major news releases unless the strategy is specifically designed for that environment. Spreads can widen sharply, and fills can become erratic. Second, be selective about the pairs and sessions you trade. A liquid pair traded during an active session usually offers more stable execution than an obscure pair during a quiet one. Third, use a broker and platform that provide transparent pricing and reliable order handling, then verify performance in a demo or small live environment before scaling up. Fourth, record your actual entry and exit prices in the trading journal so you can measure slippage instead of guessing about it. That record often reveals whether poor results came from the strategy itself or from execution conditions.

It also helps to think in terms of expected friction. Every strategy has an implicit assumption about how much spread, slippage, and delay it can tolerate while still remaining profitable. A swing trade targeting a larger move may absorb a slightly wider spread more easily than a scalping approach that depends on a small intraday edge. A breakout strategy may accept occasional slippage because the move it seeks can be large enough to justify the cost, while a range strategy may need tighter execution because its profit target is smaller. This is why execution quality should be evaluated alongside risk-to-reward and not after them. If the average cost of entering and exiting is too high relative to the target, the strategy may be structurally weak even if the chart setup looks sound.

The trader's goal is not to eliminate slippage, spreads, or execution variability, because that is not realistic. The goal is to understand them well enough that they do not quietly erode the edge. When costs are anticipated, measured, and built into the plan, they become manageable business expenses rather than hidden surprises. That mindset keeps the focus where it belongs: on whether the trade idea still makes sense after real-world market conditions are accounted for.

CHAPTER 9

Chapter 9: Trading Psychology and Emotional Control

Trading psychology is what determines whether a valid method can be applied consistently when the pressure of real money, rapid price movement, and uncertainty are all present at once. The market does not simply test a setup; it tests the trader's ability to stay aligned with a plan when emotions are pushing for speed, certainty, or relief. That is why the next part of the book shifts from technique to self-management. A trader can know the rules for entries, exits, and risk and still undermine them through impatience, hesitation, or the urge to interfere once a position is open.

Recognizing emotional triggers that lead to poor trading decisions

Emotional triggers rarely announce themselves as emotions. More often, they show up as a sudden urge to act: to enter because the move feels urgent, to exit because a small pullback feels threatening, or to increase size because the last trade "should have" worked. The first step in controlling them is learning to identify the conditions that reliably push your judgment off course. For many traders, the trigger is not the chart itself but the meaning they attach to it. A fast breakout can feel like a rare opportunity that must not be missed. A losing streak can feel like proof that the method is broken. A profitable run can feel like evidence that risk no longer matters. Once price becomes tied to personal validation, the trader stops evaluating the setup and starts reacting to the emotional story around it.

One of the most common triggers is the need to recover quickly from discomfort. A trader who has just taken a loss may feel an immediate pull to reenter the market, not because a clear setup has appeared, but because the loss created tension that needs relief. That tension can produce revenge trading, but it can also produce more subtle mistakes: widening a stop to avoid being wrong again, taking a lower-quality entry because waiting feels frustrating, or closing a valid winner too early just to reduce uncertainty. These reactions are especially dangerous because they often feel rational in the moment. The trader tells himself that he is being flexible or decisive, when in fact he is trying to escape the emotional weight of the previous trade.

Another trigger is overattachment to being right. Some traders do not simply want to make money; they want the market to confirm their analysis. That creates a hidden vulnerability. If price moves against the idea, the trader may defend the position longer than the plan allows. If price moves in the expected direction, the trader may become attached to the outcome and ignore signs that momentum is fading. In both cases, the issue is not the setup itself but the ego investment behind it. The more a trader treats a trade as a verdict on personal skill, the harder it becomes to make clean decisions. A professional mindset requires separating the quality of the process from the outcome of any single position.

Excitement is another powerful trigger, especially in fast-moving forex conditions where volatility can make every candle feel important. Sudden momentum can create a sense of urgency that overrides patience. Traders begin to chase candles, enter before confirmation, or add positions simply because price is moving quickly. This is one reason highly gamified trading environments can be so difficult to resist; they reward rapid action and constant engagement [52]. In practice, excitement often leads to the same error as fear: it narrows attention. Instead of asking whether the setup still fits the plan, the trader focuses on the possibility of missing out. That shift from evaluation to impulse is often the point at which discipline starts to break down.

Loss aversion also deserves special attention because it can distort behavior in both directions. After a loss, some traders become overly cautious and begin avoiding valid opportunities. Others become more aggressive, increasing size to "make back" what was lost. Both responses are attempts to restore emotional balance rather than to follow the trading plan. Behavioral research on financial decision-making consistently shows that psychological factors can alter judgment in ways that are not obvious to the person making the decision [168]. In trading, that means the danger is not only in obvious panic. It is also in the quieter forms of bias that make a trader hesitate, overtrade, or force a decision simply to reduce internal pressure.

The practical way to recognize triggers is to watch for patterns in your own behavior, not just in the market. If you notice that you trade differently after a win than after a loss, or that certain times of day make you more impatient, those are not random moods. They are conditions that need to be managed. A trader might discover, for example, that news-driven volatility makes him chase entries, or that a series of small losses makes him abandon his stop-loss rules. Another trader may find that boredom is the real trigger, leading to unnecessary trades during quiet sessions. Once the pattern is visible, it becomes easier to design rules around it: stepping away after a loss, reducing size during emotional periods, or requiring a longer checklist before entering a trade.

The goal is not to eliminate emotion, which is unrealistic, but to detect when emotion has begun to steer the decision. A useful question before every trade is simple: am I responding to the market, or am I responding to how the market makes me feel? If the answer is the second, the trade deserves extra scrutiny. Traders who build this habit become better at recognizing the early warning signs: a faster heartbeat, a stronger urge to "do something," a need to prove a point, or a sudden disregard for normal filters. Those signals are often more revealing than the chart itself. When you can identify the trigger before it becomes action, you create the pause needed for discipline to reenter the process.

Building habits that support patience, focus, and objectivity

Patience, focus, and objectivity are not traits that appear only when a trader "gets better." They are habits built through repeated choices that make impulsive behavior harder and disciplined behavior easier. In practice, that means designing your trading day so you are not constantly negotiating with yourself. If you sit down with no plan for when to look at charts, when to stop analyzing, or when to step away, the market will keep offering reasons to act. The more often you react, the less room you leave for deliberate judgment.

Patience begins with accepting that not every valid market condition is worth trading. A trader who feels pressure to participate in every session usually confuses activity with progress. One useful habit is to define in advance what type of setup deserves attention and then treat everything else as noise. That simple rule reduces the temptation to force a trade just because price is moving. It also makes waiting feel purposeful rather than passive. Waiting is not doing nothing; it is preserving capital and attention for conditions that match the plan.

Focus is easier to maintain when it is limited. Many traders damage their concentration by watching too many pairs, checking too many time frames, or refreshing charts every few minutes in search of a new opportunity. A narrower watchlist creates a cleaner mental environment.

It allows you to become familiar with the normal behavior of the instruments you trade, which makes unusual behavior easier to detect. It also reduces the mental fatigue that comes from constant switching. When your attention is scattered, you are more likely to mistake novelty for quality.

Objectivity depends on separating observation from interpretation. A chart should first tell you what price is doing, not what you hope it will do. That sounds basic, but hope is often the first bias to enter the process. A trader may want a breakout to continue, a reversal to appear, or a losing position to recover, and those preferences can quietly distort the reading of evidence. One way to protect objectivity is to use written criteria before entry and to review the chart against those criteria after the fact. If the setup no longer meets the rules, the trade idea should be revised or abandoned, even if the emotional part of you wants a different outcome.

Another helpful habit is to introduce a pause between impulse and action. This does not have to be dramatic. It can be as simple as checking the setup against a short pre-trade list, waiting for the candle to close, or requiring a second look at the higher time frame before committing. The point is to slow down enough for judgment to catch up with emotion. Behavioral research on investment decision-making consistently shows that psychological factors can distort choices when people rely on quick reactions instead of structured evaluation [168]. Trading is no exception. A small delay can be enough to prevent a trade from being entered because of urgency rather than edge.

Physical environment matters more than many traders expect. A cluttered desk, constant notifications, multiple open tabs, and a phone within easy reach all encourage distraction. A cleaner workspace supports cleaner thinking. The same is true of routine. If you begin each session the same way—reviewing the plan, checking the calendar, marking levels, and confirming risk limits—you reduce the number of decisions that must be made under pressure. Repetition is valuable because it turns discipline into default behavior. Over time, the routine itself becomes a cue for calm, methodical thinking.

Objectivity also improves when you measure yourself by process rather than by the emotional tone of the day. A trader can feel frustrated and still execute well, or feel confident and still make poor decisions. Because feelings are unreliable performance metrics, they should not be used to judge whether a session was successful. Instead, ask whether you followed the plan, respected risk, and waited for valid conditions. That standard keeps the focus on what you can control. It also makes it easier to recognize when impatience, distraction, or bias is beginning to influence decisions before those habits become costly.

Recovering from losses without abandoning the trading plan

Losses are part of trading, but the way a trader responds to them determines whether they remain normal business expenses or become the start of a damaging spiral. The first discipline is to separate the outcome of a single trade from the quality of the plan that produced it. A well-formed setup can still lose because the market does not owe immediate follow-through, and a poorly formed setup can sometimes win by accident. If you judge yourself only by the last result, you will eventually reward bad process and punish good process. That is how traders start changing rules after every setback, which usually creates more inconsistency than the loss itself.

Recovering well begins before the next trade is considered. After a losing position, the trader needs a pause long enough to reduce emotional momentum and restore objectivity. That does not mean avoiding the market indefinitely; it means refusing to make the next decision while still carrying the emotional charge of the last one. A short break, a review of the original setup, and a check against the written plan can prevent the common impulse to "fix" the loss with a faster, larger, or more aggressive trade. The market often invites that reaction because it keeps moving, but urgency is not the same as opportunity.

One useful habit is to review the loss in terms of execution quality rather than profit and loss alone. Ask whether the entry matched the plan, whether the stop was placed where the setup was invalidated, whether the position size was appropriate, and whether the trade was exited for the right reason. If the answers are yes, then the loss may simply be the cost of participation in a probabilistic system. If the answers are no, then the correction should target the specific rule that was broken, not the entire strategy. This distinction matters because traders often abandon a valid method after a few normal losses, while overlooking the real issue: they were not following the method consistently enough for it to work.

It also helps to expect that losses can cluster. Even a strategy with a genuine edge can experience a rough stretch because market conditions change, volatility expands or contracts, or the pair being traded enters a phase that does not suit the method. A trader who understands this is less likely to interpret a drawdown as proof of failure. The correct response is to compare current conditions with the conditions the strategy was designed for. If the environment has shifted, the answer may be to reduce activity or stand aside temporarily, not to rewrite the plan in the middle of a slump.

Another common mistake is trying to recover emotionally before recovering statistically. Traders often feel pressure to "get back to even," but breakeven is not a market signal. It is a psychological target that can encourage oversized positions, premature entries, and unnecessary trades. A better approach is to focus on process recovery first: trade only valid setups, keep risk per trade unchanged, and let a sequence of disciplined decisions rebuild confidence. Confidence that comes from process is more durable than confidence that comes from one lucky win after a loss. The market can take that confidence away just as quickly if it was never grounded in rules.

When the loss is large enough to affect concentration, the trader should reduce exposure until decision-making feels steady again. That may mean cutting position size, limiting the number of trades for a few sessions, or restricting activity to only the highest-quality setups. This is not a sign of weakness. It is a way of preventing frustration from turning into revenge trading or careless rule-bending. Behavioral research on private investors consistently shows that psychological pressure can distort judgment and push people toward poorer decisions when emotions are high [168]. In trading, the practical answer is to make the next choice smaller, simpler, and easier to execute correctly.

There is also value in treating recovery as a structured process rather than an emotional event. A trader can define a reset routine that includes reviewing the losing trade, checking whether the loss fits within normal expectancy, confirming that no rule was violated, and writing down the one lesson that should affect the next decision. If the trade was valid, the lesson may simply be to continue. If the trade exposed a flaw in timing, risk placement, or patience, then the correction should be specific and measurable. That approach keeps a setback from becoming a story about personal failure. It turns the loss into information, which is exactly what a professional trading process requires.

Finally, recovery means preserving the trading plan long enough for it to prove itself. One loss, or even a short series of losses, is not enough data to justify abandoning a method that has been tested and applied consistently. The trader's job is not to avoid discomfort; it is to stay disciplined through it. That discipline is what keeps temporary adversity from becoming permanent damage. When the plan is sound, the response to a loss is not reinvention. It is controlled continuation.

Journaling and self-review as tools for psychological improvement

Journaling is useful only when it records the truth of your trading process, not the version of events you wish had happened. A good journal captures the setup, the reason for taking the trade, the risk defined before entry, the emotions present at the time, and the actual decisions made while the trade was live. That record turns vague experience into something you can study. Without it, most traders remember the outcome and forget the process. With it, patterns begin to emerge: you may notice that losses cluster around certain sessions, that impulsive entries happen after long periods of inactivity, or that your best trades come when you follow a narrow set of conditions and do not interfere. The journal is not there to prove that you are disciplined. It is there to show where discipline is strong and where it breaks down.

The most useful entries are usually simple and consistent. Before the trade, note the pair, time frame, direction, setup type, entry trigger, stop-loss level, target, and position size. Also record the reason the trade fits your plan. During or after the trade, note whether you followed the plan exactly, whether you moved the stop, whether you exited early, and what you were feeling when those decisions were made. Traders often skip the emotional part because it feels subjective, but emotional context is one of the clearest clues to recurring mistakes. If you can see that you tend to rush when you are bored, widen stops when you are anxious, or overtrade after a win, you can address the real problem instead of only its financial result.

Self-review becomes more effective when it is tied to categories rather than isolated memories. At the end of a session or week, sort your trades into groups such as valid setup, invalid setup, rule-following loss, rule-breaking loss, and rule-breaking win. That last category matters because a profitable violation can quietly train bad habits. A trader who rewards a lucky trade may begin to trust behavior that would be harmful over a larger sample. Reviewing trades this way separates outcome from execution. It also reveals whether your edge is being reduced by avoidable errors. A strategy that should be profitable can appear weak if the trader repeatedly enters late, sizes too large, or exits before the market has room to work.

Effective review asks specific questions. Did I take only the setups my plan allows? Did I enter for the right reason or because I felt pressure to act? Did I honor the stop-loss exactly as planned? Did I change the trade because new information justified it, or because I wanted to avoid discomfort? Did I increase risk after a loss or after a win? These questions are important because they expose the difference between judgment and impulse. Over time, the answers form a behavioral profile. That profile can be more valuable than a simple profit-and-loss report because it shows the habits driving the numbers. A trader who knows the source of repeated errors can correct them more efficiently than one who only sees a losing month and assumes the whole method is broken.

It helps to review your journal on two levels. The first level is mechanical: were the rules followed, were the entries aligned with the plan, and was risk controlled properly? The second level is psychological: what mindset showed up before, during, and after the trade? A trader may execute mechanically well while still carrying frustration, overconfidence, or hesitation into the next decision. Those states matter because they influence the next trade even when the current one is closed. If you notice that a loss tends to trigger revenge behavior, the review should not simply label the trade as bad. It should identify the emotional sequence that followed the loss and the point at which the plan was abandoned. That is where improvement begins.

Written review is especially valuable because it creates accountability across time. Memory changes after the fact. A losing trade may later feel smaller than it was, and a winning trade may feel more skillful than it actually was. A journal protects you from those distortions. It also gives you evidence when your confidence is low. If you are following the plan and the results are temporarily weak, the journal can show that the issue may be variance rather than poor execution. That distinction helps prevent emotional overcorrection, such as abandoning a valid method after a normal drawdown. At the same time, the journal can keep you honest when results are good for the wrong reasons. Consistent note-taking makes it harder to confuse luck with skill.

Some traders benefit from a short daily debrief and a longer weekly review. The daily review should be quick: what was done well, what was done poorly, and what must be adjusted tomorrow. The weekly review can be deeper, looking for repeated mistakes, recurring emotional triggers, and the conditions under which the best trades occurred. Recent research in financial forecasting and algorithmic methods has emphasized the value of structured data and systematic pattern recognition in decision-making [81] [98] [75]. Trading journals serve a similar purpose for the individual trader: they turn scattered experience into structured information that can be examined, compared, and improved. The goal is not to write more. The goal is to see more clearly what your trading is actually doing.

CHAPTER 10

Chapter 10: Developing a Sustainable Trading Routine

A sustainable routine is what turns trading from a series of isolated decisions into a repeatable process that can be evaluated, improved, and maintained over time. Without structure, even a trader with sound analysis and solid risk rules can drift into inconsistency: checking charts too often, taking marginal setups, or letting one session dictate the mood for the next. A routine does not eliminate uncertainty, but it does create a dependable framework for handling it. It helps separate preparation from execution, and execution from review, so each part of the trading process has its place instead of competing for attention at the same moment.

Pre-market preparation and scanning for high-quality setups

Pre-market preparation begins before the first trade setup appears. The goal is not to predict the day, but to narrow the field so you know which markets deserve attention and which ones should be ignored. A trader who starts the session by scanning every pair on the platform is usually reacting to noise, not opportunity. A better approach is to begin with a short watchlist built from the pairs that match your trading plan, then check whether current conditions still support the style you trade. That means reviewing the higher-time-frame context, the scheduled news calendar, and the current session environment before looking for entries on the lower time frame. When those pieces are aligned, the chart scan becomes far more efficient because you are searching for a specific kind of opportunity instead of trying to force one.

The first filter is market context. A pair may look active, but activity alone does not make it tradable. You want to know whether price is trending, ranging, compressing, or sitting just ahead of a major catalyst. If your method works best in directional conditions, then pairs that are trapped in a wide, messy range should be set aside. If you trade mean reversion or range boundaries, then a pair already breaking structure on the higher time frame may no longer fit your edge. This kind of filtering saves time and reduces the temptation to take trades simply because a chart is moving. The best setups are usually not the most dramatic ones; they are the ones that fit the market environment your strategy was designed for.

Once the context is clear, the next step is to scan for structure that can support a trade. That usually means looking for clean levels, orderly pullbacks, compression near a key area, or a clear rejection of a price zone that has already proven important. The purpose of the scan is not to find a signal on every chart, but to identify where one might develop if price behaves as expected. Many traders make the mistake of treating a chart scan like a search for certainty. In practice, you are looking for quality, which often means fewer opportunities, not more. A setup should have enough room to work, enough clarity to define risk, and enough alignment with the larger picture to justify attention.

It also helps to think in terms of event risk. A technically attractive setup can become poor if a major release is minutes away and the trade would be exposed to a burst of volatility that has nothing to do with the pattern itself. Pre-market preparation should include checking the economic calendar for events that could distort price, widen spreads, or create erratic movement. This is especially important when the pair is tied to a currency with a known policy announcement, inflation release, labor report, or central bank speech. If the event is likely to dominate price action, the trade may need to be delayed, reduced in size, or removed from the watchlist altogether. Discipline here is not about avoiding all news; it is about refusing to let unplanned volatility define your execution.

A useful scan also includes liquidity and timing. The same setup can behave differently depending on whether it appears near session open, during a quiet mid-session stretch, or just before a major market handoff. Some pairs move best when London volume arrives, others when New York joins the flow, and some are simply too thin outside their active hours. If your strategy depends on follow-through, you want the market to be active enough to confirm the move without forcing you into poor fills. If your method is built around slower, more deliberate movement, you may prefer times when price is less likely to whip around on transient order flow. The point is not to trade more often during busy periods, but to trade when the market conditions match the behavior your setup needs.

As you scan, keep the number of candidates small enough to manage well. A watchlist with too many pairs creates a hidden cost: it encourages comparison instead of judgment. Traders begin flipping from chart to chart, looking for the cleanest-looking move, and that process often leads to late entries or inconsistent standards. A better routine is to rank the charts by quality. Which pair has the clearest structure? Which one has the cleanest higher-time-frame bias? Which one offers enough distance to the next obstacle to justify the risk? Which one still has room before a major event? By asking the same questions every day, you create a repeatable filter instead of relying on mood or impulse.

The final part of pre-market preparation is mental, not technical. Before the session starts, you should already know what conditions make you a buyer, what conditions make you a seller, and what conditions mean no trade at all. That clarity keeps the scan honest. If you are tired, distracted, or eager to make up for yesterday, the market will offer plenty of excuses to override your standards. Preparation protects you from that drift. It gives you a structured way to begin the day: review the calendar, assess the higher time frame, narrow the watchlist, mark the key levels, and wait for price to come to you. In a business where patience is part of the edge, the quality of the scan often determines the quality of the trade.

Creating a trading journal and performance review process

A trading journal is most useful when it records decisions in a way that can be reviewed objectively later. The point is not to create a diary of feelings or a list of wins and losses, but to preserve the logic behind each trade while it is still fresh. A chart screenshot alone will not tell you why you entered, what you noticed, what you ignored, or whether you followed your own rules. A strong journal captures the full decision chain: the market context, the setup, the entry trigger, the stop placement, the target, the size, and the reason the trade was taken at all. That record becomes the raw material for improvement. Without it, you are left with impressions, and impressions are unreliable when money is on the line.

The best journal format is simple enough that you will actually use it after every trade. At a minimum, each entry should include the pair traded, date and time, session, direction, setup type, entry price, stop-loss, take-profit, position size, and result in pips and account percentage. It should also include a brief note on whether the trade followed the plan exactly or whether something was improvised. If you want the journal to be more useful, add a few qualitative fields: whether the market was trending or ranging, whether news was nearby, whether the trade was taken with confidence or hesitation, and whether the exit was planned or emotional. These details help separate a good process from a lucky outcome. A profitable trade that violated your rules is not the same as a profitable trade executed correctly, and a losing trade taken according to plan is not the same as a mistake.

Consistency matters more than complexity. Many traders begin with too many categories and then stop recording because the process feels burdensome. A better approach is to keep the journal lean enough to maintain during active trading, then expand the review layer afterward. One practical structure is to separate the journal into two parts: the trade record and the performance notes. The trade record is factual and completed immediately after the trade closes. The performance notes are written later, when you can think more clearly. That second layer is where you identify whether the setup met your criteria, whether the risk was appropriate, and whether execution matched the original plan. This distinction prevents the common mistake of judging a trade only by its profit or loss.

A performance review should focus on patterns, not isolated events. Looking at one trade tells you very little; looking at twenty or fifty trades begins to reveal how you actually trade. Over time, you can measure your average risk-to-reward, win rate, expectancy, and drawdown behavior, but those numbers are only useful if they are tied to the quality of your decisions. For example, if your journal shows that most losses come from trades taken outside your plan, the problem is not the market. If your best results come from one setup during one session, that may indicate where your edge is strongest. If your average win is too small relative to your average loss, the issue may be exit discipline rather than entry selection. The review process should answer specific questions: Which setups are worth repeating? Which conditions reduce performance? Which mistakes appear most often? Which habits protect the account?

It helps to review performance on more than one schedule. A quick daily review should confirm that each trade was logged correctly and that any rule violation is noted while memory is still accurate. A weekly review should look for recurring behavior across the recent sample and compare results to the trading plan. A monthly review should be more analytical, using a larger set of trades to evaluate whether the strategy is still being executed well and whether market conditions have changed enough to affect performance. This layered approach keeps you from overreacting to a single bad day and also prevents small problems from accumulating unnoticed. Traders often assume they need a new strategy when they actually need a better review process.

When reviewing trades, the most valuable habit is to classify outcomes by process quality. A simple label such as A, B, or C can be effective. An A trade fully met the plan, was sized correctly, and was managed according to rules. A B trade had some minor imperfection but was still acceptable. A C trade was taken with clear rule violations, poor timing, or emotional pressure. This grading system keeps the review focused on execution quality rather than on whether the market happened to move in your favor. If your account is growing but most trades are C trades, the growth may not be sustainable. If your account is flat but the majority of trades are A trades, the issue may be edge development rather than discipline. The journal should help you distinguish those cases.

Charts and screenshots are especially useful when they are attached to the written record. A trade review becomes much stronger when you can see the setup exactly as it appeared at the time of decision, not as it looks after the fact. Mark the entry, stop, target, and the reason the setup qualified. If the trade was taken from a higher-time-frame level or in response to a news-driven move, note that as well. Over time, this creates a visual archive of your decision-making. You may discover that certain patterns look attractive in hindsight but were actually low quality in real time, or that your best trades share a specific structure you had not formally recognized. That kind of discovery is one of the main advantages of disciplined journaling, and it is a practical way to refine a strategy without guessing.

The final purpose of the review process is accountability. A journal should make it difficult to pretend that a bad habit does not exist. If you repeatedly move stops, chase entries, or ignore your own filters, the record should make that impossible to deny. At the same time, it should also show when you are improving, because progress in trading is often gradual and easy to overlook. The trader who reviews honestly is better positioned to adjust size, refine setup criteria, and strengthen discipline based on evidence rather than emotion. In that sense, the journal is not merely a record of trades; it is a record of how your trading method is evolving and how well you are able to apply it under real market conditions.

Weekly analysis, strategy refinement, and lesson tracking

A weekly review works best when it is treated as a structured decision process, not a casual look back at a few charts. The purpose is to identify whether your trading decisions were aligned with your plan, whether market conditions matched the strategy you used, and whether the results came from execution quality or from a temporary market condition that will not repeat. In other words, the review is not just about what happened; it is about whether the logic behind your trades was sound. That distinction matters because a trader can have a profitable week while still making poor decisions, or have a losing week while following a valid process. A disciplined review focuses on the quality of the process first and the outcome second.

Start by separating the week into categories that make the data easier to interpret. Group trades by setup type, currency pair, session, and time frame if those variables affect your decisions. Then note which trades were taken exactly according to plan, which trades were taken with partial rule changes, and which trades were clearly outside the plan. This simple sorting often reveals more than the profit and loss column alone. If one setup type consistently performs better than others, that does not automatically mean it should be traded more aggressively; it may mean it deserves more attention because it fits current volatility or market structure. If a certain pair or session produces repeated mistakes, the issue may be your timing, your patience, or your inability to read conditions in that environment.

A useful weekly review also looks at market context. Ask whether the week was trending, range-bound, news-driven, or unusually quiet, and compare that environment with the strategy you used. A method designed for directional continuation will often struggle in choppy conditions, while a range approach may underperform when a pair is breaking into a sustained move. This is where traders often misread their results. They assume the strategy failed when the real problem was that the strategy was applied outside its intended context. Decision support research in financial trading emphasizes the value of using logical rules and structured analysis when evaluating outcomes, because the quality of the decision framework often matters more than any single result [183]. The weekly review is where that framework is tested against reality.

Strategy refinement should be based on repeated evidence, not on frustration from one or two trades. If you change your rules every time a setup loses, you are not refining a strategy; you are reacting to variance. Real refinement begins by identifying patterns that appear across a meaningful sample. For example, you may discover that entries taken after a strong session open are more reliable than late-session entries, or that your stop placement is too tight when volatility expands around major releases. You may also find that your trade management is weakening the edge by cutting winners too early or holding losers too long. The goal is to make one change at a time, then observe whether that change improves the next sample of trades. If too many variables change at once, you will not know what actually improved or worsened performance.

Lesson tracking turns those observations into a usable record. A trading journal should do more than archive screenshots and outcomes. It should capture the lesson attached to each trade in a short, specific form: what the market was doing, what you expected, what you did, and what should be repeated or avoided next time. That lesson should be written in a way that can be checked later. “Be more patient” is too vague to be useful. “Wait for the pullback to hold above prior resistance before entering” is specific enough to guide future action. Over time, these notes become a personal rulebook built from your own experience rather than from theory alone.

It helps to review both execution and behavior separately. Execution questions ask whether the trade matched the setup rules: Was the entry valid? Was the stop in the right place? Was the position size correct? Behavior questions ask how you handled uncertainty: Did you move the stop because you were uncomfortable, or because the market structure changed? Did you skip valid trades after a loss? Did you overtrade after a win? This separation is important because a trade can be executed correctly even if the result is negative, and a profitable trade can still expose a weak habit that will eventually hurt performance. The job of lesson tracking is to make those habits visible before they become expensive.

A practical review process can be kept simple. At the end of each week, record the number of trades taken, the number that followed the plan, the number that did not, the setups that worked best, the setups that underperformed, and the most important behavioral mistake or improvement. Then write one adjustment for the coming week. That adjustment should be narrow enough to test, such as reducing trades during low-liquidity hours, waiting for stronger confirmation on breakouts, or limiting discretionary exits. This kind of disciplined adjustment process is consistent with real-time decision systems that rely on rules, feedback, and repeated evaluation rather than impulse [183]. Over time, the weekly record becomes a map of what you actually do under pressure, which is far more valuable than what you believe you do when reviewing trades casually.

Balancing trading with risk control, rest, and long-term consistency

Sustainable trading is built on the idea that performance is not measured by one strong week or one clean entry, but by whether your process can be repeated without wearing you down. That is why risk control cannot be separated from rest and routine. A trader who sizes positions responsibly but stays glued to the screen all day is still exposing themselves to fatigue, impatience, and decision drift. Likewise, a trader who has good discipline in theory but no structure for stepping away will eventually make choices under pressure that do not match the plan. The practical goal is to make your trading method durable enough to survive ordinary stress, not just your best moments.

One of the most common ways traders undermine consistency is by treating every market condition as if it deserves equal attention. In reality, your edge is usually tied to specific conditions: a certain session, a certain level of volatility, a trend or range environment, or a particular pair behavior. If those conditions are not present, the correct decision is often to do nothing. That restraint is not missed opportunity; it is risk control. It protects both capital and mental energy. A trader who forces trades outside their best conditions is taking on hidden costs that do not always show up in the account balance immediately, but they do show up in lower confidence, poorer execution, and more emotional interference on the next setup.

Rest matters because trading performance depends on attention, not just analysis. When you are tired, your ability to wait, compare alternatives, and follow a sequence of rules declines. You may still see the chart, but you stop seeing it clearly. That is especially dangerous in forex, where price can move quickly and the temptation to react is constant. A tired trader is more likely to widen a stop, chase an entry, or justify a marginal setup. Building rest into the routine is therefore part of the trading plan, not a personal luxury. This can mean setting a hard cutoff time for chart review, avoiding late-night market monitoring unless your style requires it, and reducing screen time after a volatile session so you can reset before the next decision cycle.

Consistency also improves when you define limits that protect you from overtrading. A daily loss limit, a maximum number of trades, or a rule that ends the session after a certain amount of emotional strain can prevent one bad stretch from becoming a full-day problem. These limits are not there because every losing streak is dangerous in itself; they are there because the quality of decision-making tends to decline once frustration takes over. In that sense, a stop for the day is similar to a stop-loss on a trade. It acknowledges that your judgment has a boundary and that crossing it creates more risk than opportunity. Traders who respect that boundary are usually more stable over time than traders who try to "make the day back."

Another part of long-term consistency is understanding that effort should be distributed across the week, not concentrated only during active trading hours. The best routine includes periods for preparation, execution, review, and recovery. Preparation means scanning the market with a clear filter rather than wandering from chart to chart. Execution means taking only the trades that fit the plan. Review means checking whether you followed your rules and whether the market conditions matched your strategy. Recovery means giving yourself enough distance from the screen to come back with objectivity. When those pieces are balanced, trading becomes more professional and less reactive. The account benefits, but so does your ability to stay patient through ordinary market uncertainty.

It also helps to think in terms of energy management rather than willpower alone. Willpower is easiest to use when you are fresh and hardest to rely on when you are mentally crowded by news, losses, or a long sequence of small decisions. A simple routine can reduce that burden: review the calendar at a fixed time, limit the number of pairs on your watchlist, and decide in advance when you will stop analyzing. By narrowing the number of decisions you need to make each day, you preserve focus for the moments that matter. Research in financial modeling and trading systems increasingly reflects the importance of regime awareness and adaptive decision-making rather than blind repetition of one method in all conditions [142][188]. For the individual trader, that means staying selective and avoiding the pressure to be active just to feel engaged.

Long-term consistency is not only about protecting yourself from mistakes; it is also about creating a pace you can sustain through changing market cycles. Some periods will reward your strategy more than others. Some weeks will require smaller size, less trading, or more patience. If your routine assumes constant opportunity, it will break when the market slows or shifts. If your routine assumes that your job is to manage risk, protect focus, and wait for qualified setups, it will remain workable across different environments. The trader who lasts is usually not the one who tries hardest to extract something from every session, but the one who can keep showing up with discipline, clear limits, and enough rest to make the next decision well.

Citations

The following sources were referenced in the preceding chapters. Each entry links back to the inline reference in the text. All sources were verified against the OpenAlex academic database at the time of generation.

1. Qiang Ji, Elie Bouri, Chi Keung Marco Lau et al. (2018). Dynamic connectedness and integration in cryptocurrency markets. https://doi.org/10.1016/j.irfa.2018.12.002

2. Zexin Hu, Yiqi Zhao, Matloob Khushi (2021). A Survey of Forex and Stock Price Prediction Using Deep Learning. https://doi.org/10.3390/asi4010009

3. Bruce Vanstone, Gavin Finnie (2008). An empirical methodology for developing stockmarket trading systems using artificial neural networks. https://doi.org/10.1016/j.eswa.2008.08.019

4. Marcel Fratzscher, Oliver Gloede, Lukas Menkhoff et al. (2019). When Is Foreign Exchange Intervention Effective? Evidence from 33 Countries. https://doi.org/10.1257/mac.20150317

5. Garrick Hileman, Michel Rauchs (2017). 2017 Global Blockchain Benchmarking Study. https://doi.org/10.2139/ssrn.3040224

6. Jana Doering, Renatas Kizys, Ángel A. Juan et al. (2019). Metaheuristics for rich portfolio optimisation and risk management: Current state and future trends. https://doi.org/10.1016/j.orp.2019.100121

7. Adamantios Ntakaris, Martin Magris, Juho Kanniainen et al. (2018). Benchmark dataset for mid-price forecasting of limit order book data with machine learning methods. https://doi.org/10.1002/for.2543

8. Michael R. King, Carol L. Osler, Dagfinn Rime (2012). Foreign Exchange Market Structure, Players, and Evolution. https://doi.org/10.1002/9781118445785.ch1

9. Jozef Baruník, Tomáš Křehlík, Lukáš Vácha (2015). Modeling and forecasting exchange rate volatility in time-frequency domain. https://doi.org/10.1016/j.ejor.2015.12.010

10. Emily Fletcher, Charles Larkin, Shaen Corbet (2021). Countering money laundering and terrorist financing: A case for bitcoin regulation. https://doi.org/10.1016/j.ribaf.2021.101387

11. Abderahman Rejeb, Karim Rejeb, John G. Keogh (2021). Cryptocurrencies in Modern Finance: A Literature Review. https://doi.org/10.15408/etk.v20i1.16911

12. Bilal Hassan Ahmed Khattak, Imran Shafi, Abdul Saboor Khan et al. (2023). A Systematic Survey of AI Models in Financial Market Forecasting for Profitability Analysis. https://doi.org/10.1109/access.2023.3330156

13. Darko Vuković, Senanu Dekpo-Adza, Stefana Matović (2025). AI integration in financial services: a systematic review of trends and regulatory challenges. https://doi.org/10.1057/s41599-025-04850-8

14. Setsuya Sato, Helen Allen, John Hawkins (2002). Electronic trading and its implications for financial systems. https://doi.org/10.4324/9780203222614.ch12

15. Helen Allen, John Hawkins, Setsuya Sato (2002). Electronic trading and its implications for financial systems. https://doi.org/10.4324/9780203222614-24

16. Theo Lynn, John G. Mooney, Pierangelo Rosati et al. (2020). Measuring the Business Value of Cloud Computing. https://doi.org/10.1007/978-3-030-43198-3

17. Divya Singh, Aditya Keshari, Amit Gautam (2024). International trade and investment: A review and research agenda. https://doi.org/10.1002/joe.22254

18. David Jukl, Jan Lánský (2025). Systematic Review on Algorithmic Trading. https://doi.org/10.18267/j.aip.276

19. Rui Pedro Barbosa (2011). Agents in the market place an exploratory study on using intelligent agents to trade financial instruments. https://openalex.org/W129294831

20. Luís Lobato Macedo (2018). An Inquiry into the Validity of Technical Analysis in Financial Markets With the Use of Evolutionary Techniques. https://openalex.org/W2888195128

21. Bruce Mizrach, Christopher J. Neely (2006). The Transition to Electronic Communications Networks in the Secondary Treasury Market. https://doi.org/10.20955/r.88.527-542

22. Julien Chevallier, Dominique Guégan, Stéphane Goutte (2021). Is It Possible to Forecast the Price of Bitcoin?. https://doi.org/10.3390/forecast3020024

23. Alfonso Guarino, Luca Grilli, Domenico Santoro et al. (2022). To learn or not to learn? Evaluating autonomous, adaptive, automated traders in cryptocurrencies financial bubbles. https://doi.org/10.1007/s00521-022-07543-4

24. Aleksandr P. Alekseenko (2023). Model Framework for Consumer Protection and Crypto-Exchanges Regulation. https://doi.org/10.3390/jrfm16070305

25. Chikako Baba, Cristina Batog, Enrique Flores et al. (2020). Fintech in Europe. https://doi.org/10.5089/9781513561165.001

26. Servaas Storm (2022). Inflation in the Time of Corona and War: The plight of the developing economies. https://doi.org/10.36687/inet-wp192

27. Rim El Bernoussi, Michael Rockinger (2022). Rebalancing with transaction costs: theory, simulations, and actual data. https://doi.org/10.1007/s11408-022-00419-6

28. Mikhail Vyacheslavovich Zharikov (2023). Digital Money Options for the BRICS. https://doi.org/10.3390/ijfs11010042

29. Wael Dammak (2023). Evaluation des options sur devises en présence des coûts d'information statiques et dynamiques : modèles théoriques et validation empirique. https://openalex.org/W4405770230

30. Forrest Carter Cinelli, Klaudia Linek, Sean William Doncaster et al. (2016). Expanding on the 10 O'Clock Bulls. https://openalex.org/W2947642773

31. Salman Bahoo, Marco Cucculelli, Xhoana Goga et al. (2024). Artificial intelligence in Finance: a comprehensive review through bibliometric and content analysis. https://doi.org/10.1007/s43546-023-00618-x

32. Alexandra Horobeţ, Sabri Boubaker, Lucian Belaşcu et al. (2024). Technology-driven advancements: Mapping the landscape of algorithmic trading literature. https://doi.org/10.1016/j.techfore.2024.123746

33. Melvin D. Ayogu (1997). Empirical studies of Nigeria's foreign exchange parallel market II: speculative efficiency and noisy trading. https://openalex.org/W2162145357

34. P. S. Aithal, Vinay V. Prabhu (2025). The Evolution of Banking Industry in India: Past, Present, and Future with Special Emphasis on the Impact of AI on Banking Operations. https://doi.org/10.64818/pijtrcs.3107.8494.0018

35. Schlomit Azgad-Tromer (2018). Crypto Securities: On the Risks of Investments in Blockchain-Based Assets and the Dilemmas of Securities Regulation. https://openalex.org/W2937383884

36. David Bicchetti, Nicolas Maystre (2013). The synchronized and long-lasting structural change on commodity markets: Evidence from high frequency data. https://doi.org/10.3233/af-13028

37. Long Chen (2007). Price discovery in the foreign exchange market. https://openalex.org/W755668461

38. Jamari Markus, Baku Agyo Raphael, Ismaila Jesse Mazadu (2025). Automated Forex Trading Bot Using MQL4: A Reinforcement Learning-based Approach. https://doi.org/10.11648/j.acis.20251303.11

39. Bushirat T. Bolarinwa, Haruna Umar Yahaya, M. U. Adehi et al. (2025). MODELING JUMPS IN INTRADAILY FINANCIAL DATA: A REVIEW OF METHODS AND APPLICATIONS. https://doi.org/10.70382/tijsrat.v09i9.055

40. Joseph, Doniya (2025). Comparing Trading Strategies in Cryptocurrency and Traditional Asset Markets : Risk-Return Analysis with a Focus on Elliott Wave Theory and Empirical Distributions. https://openalex.org/W7112578622

41. Xiangguang Xiao (2009). High frequency trading system design and process management. https://openalex.org/W1588577865

42. Francisco López Herrera, Jaime González Maiz Jiménez, Adán Reyes Santiago (2025). Directional forecasting for eight forex pairs against the US dollar using machine learning techniques. https://doi.org/10.1007/s44163-025-00424-4

43. Sebastian Jansen (2011). Testing market imperfections via genetic programming. https://openalex.org/W1727571560

44. Rejon Kumar Ray (2025). MULTI-MARKET FINANCIAL CRISIS PREDICTION: A MACHINE LEARNING APPROACH US-

ING STOCK, BOND, AND FOREX DATA. https://doi.org/10.12732/ijam.v38i8s.602

45. International Monetary Fund (2004). Pakistan: Selected Issues and Statistical Appendix. https://doi.org/10.5089/9781451830644.002

46. Siddiqui, Ariba Rehan (2025). A novel hybrid decision making framework for FX hedging strategy selection using machine learning and fuzzy TOPSIS. https://openalex.org/W7114946050

47. Chuku Chuku (n.d.). Essays on Economic Policies for Resource-Rich Developing Economies. https://openalex.org/W7127554269

48. Yves Sagaert, Nikolaos Kourentzes, El-Houssaine Aghezzaf et al. (2014). Demand forecasting using exogenous leading indicators. https://openalex.org/W2580166129

49. Henry T. C. Hu, Peter L. Bernstein (1993). Misunderstood Derivatives: The Causes of Informational Failure and the Promise of Regulatory Incrementalism. https://doi.org/10.2307/796975

50. Xiao-Yang Liu, Ziyi Xia, Hongyang Yang et al. (2024). Dynamic datasets and market environments for financial reinforcement learning. https://doi.org/10.1007/s10994-023-06511-w

51. Pier Giuseppe Giribone (2023). Notes on Quantitative Financial Analysis. https://doi.org/10.47473/2016eda0001

52. Nizan Geslevich Packin, Doron Kliger, Amnon Reichman et al. (2025). Hooked and Hustled: The Predatory Allure of Gamblified Finance. https://doi.org/10.52214/cblr.v2025i1.14252

53. Craig Allen Nesbitt, Mariela Qirici, Jonathan Baiden et al. (2013). FOREX Trading and Investment. https://openalex.org/W3093926598

54. Richard Ramyar (2006). Essays on technical analysis in financial markets. https://doi.org/10.13140/rg.2.2.34063.33446

55. Xiao-Yang Liu, Ziyi Xia, Hongyang Yang et al. (2023). Dynamic Datasets and Market Environments for Financial Reinforcement Learning. https://doi.org/10.48550/arxiv.2304.13174

56. Thomas Chinwe Urama (2018). Stochastic calculus and derivatives pricing in the Nigerian stock market. https://doi.org/10.7190/shu-thesis-00108

57. Andrii Beliak (2023). Book of abstracts. https://doi.org/10.36690/iccm-2023

58. Ahmet Murat Ozbayoglu, Mehmet Ugur Gudelek, Ömer Berat Sezer (2020). Deep learning for financial applications : A survey. https://doi.org/10.1016/j.asoc.2020.106384

59. Arif Perdana, Hee Jhee Jiow (2024). Crypto-Cognitive Exploitation: Integrating Cognitive, Social, and Technological perspectives on cryptocurrency fraud. https://doi.org/10.1016/j.tele.2024.102191

60. Stephen A. Deane, Olivier Fines (2023). Cryptoassets: Beyond the Hype. https://doi.org/10.56227/23.1.1

61. Simone Giansante (2012). Reserve Bank of India - Financial Stability Report: June 2012. https://openalex.org/W1485304152

62. Nasser Zain Al-Abidin Ahmed, Mr Suhael, Chandan Chavadi et al. (2024). Two Day National Seminar on India's $5 Trillion Economy: The Vision, Challenges, and Roadmap [5te-2024]. https://doi.org/10.34293/india-5te-2024

63. Shamaila Butt (2025). Dual Neural Paradigm: GRU-LSTM Hybrid for Precision Exchange Rate Predictions. https://doi.org/10.14569/ijacsa.2025.01604100

64. Alan M. Taylor, Mark P. Taylor (2004). The Purchasing Power Parity Debate. https://doi.org/10.1257/0895330042632744

65. Anton Kajtazi, Andrea Moro (2018). The role of bitcoin in well diversified portfolios: A comparative global study. https://doi.org/10.1016/j.irfa.2018.10.003

66. Ricardo J. Caballero, Emmanuel Farhi, Pierre-Olivier Gourinchas (2006). An Equilibrum Model of 'Global Imbalances' and Low Interest Rates. https://doi.org/10.2139/ssrn.1012292

67. Francesco Rundo, Francesca Trenta, Agatino Luigi di Stallo et al. (2019). Machine Learning for Quantitative Finance Applications: A Survey. https://doi.org/10.3390/app9245574

68. Saeede Anbaee Farimani, Majid Vafaei Jahan, Amin Milani Fard (2022). From Text Representation to Financial Market Prediction: A Literature Review. https://doi.org/10.3390/info13100466

69. Lei Xu (2018). Machine learning and causal analyses for modeling financial and economic data. https://doi.org/10.1186/s40535-018-0058-5

70. Michael Sager (2004). Exchange rate modelling and forecasting. https://openalex.org/W1597321993

71. Ying Chen (2007). Adaptive risk management. https://doi.org/10.18452/15581

72. Lisa Marie Vachalek (2014). The Making of a Crisis in Mexico: An Inductive Analysis of Media Sentiment and Information Cascades on the Value of the Mexican Peso during the 2008 Global Financial Crisis. https://openalex.org/W765188246

73. Alan Fernandez, Remy Kaldawy, Zoraver Kang et al. (2019). AI Driven System of Trading Systems. https://openalex.org/W2970448025

74. Luís Almeida, Elisabete Vieira (2023). Technical Analysis, Fundamental Analysis, and Ichimoku Dynamics: A Bibliometric Analysis. https://doi.org/10.3390/risks11080142

75. Sofia Giantsidi, Claudia Tarantola (2025). Deep learning for financial forecasting: A review of recent trends. https://doi.org/10.1016/j.iref.2025.104719

76. Xinyao Wang, Lili Liu (2025). Risk-Sensitive Deep Reinforcement Learning for Portfolio Optimization. https://doi.org/10.3390/jrfm18070347

77. Mauricio Argotty-Erazo, Antonio Blázquez-Zaballos, Carlos A. Argoty-Eraso et al. (2023). A Novel Linear-Model-Based Methodology for Predicting the Directional Movement of the Euro-Dollar Exchange Rate. https://doi.org/10.1109/access.2023.3285082

78. Rune Aamodt (2010). Using Artificial Neural Networks To Forecast Financial Time Series. https://openalex.org/W129439822

79. Mohamad Alamili (2011). Exchange Rate Prediction using Support Vector Machines: A comparison with Artificial Neural Networks. https://openalex.org/W600474740

80. Reza Gharoie Ahangar, Asma Salman (2020). Investment Strategies in Emerging New Trends in Finance. https://doi.org/10.5772/intechopen.78097

81. Gil Cohen (2022). Algorithmic Trading and Financial Forecasting Using Advanced Artificial Intelligence Methodologies. https://doi.org/10.3390/math10183302

82. Adrian Millea (2021). Deep Reinforcement Learning for Trading—A Critical Survey. https://doi.org/10.3390/data6110119

83. David Alaminos, M. Belén Salas, Manuel Á. Fernández-Gámez (2023). Quantum Monte Carlo simulations for estimating FOREX markets: a speculative attacks experience. https://doi.org/10.1057/s41599-023-01836-2

84. Visalakshi Palaniappan, Iskandar Ishak, Hamidah Ibrahim et al. (2024). A Review on High-Frequency Trading Forecasting Methods: Opportunity and Challenges for Quantum Based Method. https://doi.org/10.1109/access.2024.3418458

85. Jui-Sheng Chou, Dinh-Nhat Truong, Thuy-Linh Le (2020). Interval Forecasting of Financial Time Series by Accelerated Particle

Swarm-Optimized Multi-Output Machine Learning System. https://doi.org/10.1109/access.2020.2965598

86. Shaharudin Jakpar, Michael Tinggi, Akmal Hisham Tak et al. (2018). Fundamental Analysis VS Technical analysis: The Comparison of Two Analysis in Malaysia Stock Market. https://doi.org/10.33736/uraf.1208.2018

87. Marcin Hernes, Jerzy Korczak, Dariusz Król et al. (2024). Multi-agent platform to support trading decisions in the FOREX market. https://doi.org/10.1007/s10489-024-05770-x

88. Nadeem Malibari, Iyad Katib, Rashid Mehmood (2022). Smart Robotic Strategies and Advice for Stock Trading Using Deep Transformer Reinforcement Learning. https://doi.org/10.3390/app122412526

89. Nicole Hui Lin Kan, Qi Cao, Chai Quek (2024). Learning and processing framework using Fuzzy Deep Neural Network for trading and portfolio rebalancing. https://doi.org/10.1016/j.asoc.2024.111233

90. Zineb Bousbaa, Javier Medina, Omar Bencharef (2023). Financial Time Series Forecasting: A Data Stream Mining-Based System. https://doi.org/10.3390/electronics12092039

91. Phuong Dong Nguyen, Nguyen Ngoc Thao, Duong Thi Kim et al. (2024). Deep learning-based predictive models for forex market trends: Practical implementation and performance evaluation. https://doi.org/10.1177/00368504241275370

92. Abolfazl Saghafi, Maryam Bagherian, Farhad Shokoohi (2025). Forecasting Forex EUR/USD Closing Prices Using a Dual-Input Deep Learning Model with Technical and Fundamental Indicators. https://doi.org/10.3390/math13091472

93. Watthana Pongsena, Prakaidoy Sitsayabut, Nittaya Kerdprasop et al. (2021). Development of a Model for Predicting the Direction of Daily Price Changes in the Forex Market Using Long Short-Term Memory. https://doi.org/10.18178/ijmlc.2021.11.1.1015

94. Saima Latif, Faheem Aslam, Paulo Ferreira et al. (2024). Integrating Macroeconomic and Technical Indicators into Forecasting the Stock Market: A Data-Driven Approach. https://doi.org/10.3390/economies13010006

95. Francisco J. Soltero, Pablo Fernández Blanco, J. Ignacio Hidalgo (2023). Collaborative Multiobjective Evolutionary Algorithms in the Search of Better Pareto Fronts: An Application to Trading Systems. https://doi.org/10.3390/app132212485

96. Oğuzhan Çelik (2019). Implementation of technical analysis on selected cryptocurrencies. https://openalex.org/W3167152492

97. Dušan Fister, Matjaž Perc, Timotej Jagrič (2021). Two robust long short-term memory frameworks for trading stocks. https://doi.org/10.1007/s10489-021-02249-x

98. Younes Chihab, Zineb Bousbaa, Marouane Chihab et al. (2019). Algo-Trading Strategy for Intraweek Foreign Exchange Speculation Based on Random Forest and Probit Regression. https://doi.org/10.1155/2019/8342461

99. Phumudzo Lloyd Seabe, Claude Rodrigue Bambe Moutsinga, Edson Pindza (2025). Sentiment-driven cryptocurrency forecasting: analyzing LSTM, GRU, Bi-LSTM, and temporal attention model (TAM). https://doi.org/10.1007/s13278-025-01463-6

100. Saskia ter Ellen (2010). Measurement, Dynamics, and Implications of Heterogeneous Beliefs in Financial Markets. https://openalex.org/W2158437728

101. Gregory Scopino (2014). Do Automated Trading Systems Dream of Manipulating the Price of Futures Contracts? Policing Markets for Improper Trading Practices by Algorithmic Robots. https://openalex.org/W1534682125

102. Amer Bakhach (2018). Developing trading strategies under the Directional Changes framework, with application in the FX Market. https://openalex.org/W2904453625

103. José Jeovane R. Cordeiro, Arlino Henrique M. de Araújo, Guilherme A. Avelino (2026). Scalper Major: A Computational Solution for Automated Trading in High Volatility Environments. https://doi.org/10.5753/sbsi.2026.248290

104. David Umoru, Beauty Igbinovia, Emoabino Muhammed et al. (2025). Volatility dynamics of stock returns, liquidity and exchange rates in ASEAN Countries. https://doi.org/10.5267/j.ac.2024.11.001

105. Stefano Cavestro (2017). The High Frequency Trading Phenomenon and its Influence on Capital Markets: Evidences from the Pound Flash Crash. https://openalex.org/W2762274549

106. Guglielmo Maria Caporale, Alex Plastun (2019). Price overreactions in the cryptocurrency market. https://doi.org/10.1108/jes-09-2018-0310

107. Martín Grandes, Marcel Peter, Nicolás Pinaud (2003). The Currency Premium and Local-Currency Denominated Debt Costs in South Africa. https://doi.org/10.1787/608773542458

108. World Bank (2021). Sierra Leone 2021 Economic Update. https://doi.org/10.1596/35784

109. Paloma Acevedo, Enrique Alberola Ila, Carmen Broto (2007). Local debt expansion... vulnerability reduction?: an assessment for six crisis-prone countries. https://openalex.org/W3125911893

110. Paloma Acevedo, Enrique Alberola, Carmen Broto (2007). Local debt expansion... vulnerability reduction? An assessment for six crises-prone countries. https://openalex.org/W3123908484

111. Lei Gu, Yixin Shen (2024). The Application and Accuracy of Big Data in Financial Market Forecasting. https://doi.org/10.22158/jepf.v10n4p294

112. Valtteri Vaskikari (2020). Identifying tactical asset allocation signals for US and European equities. https://openalex.org/W3172612965

113. Václav Hausenblas, Vojtěch Pištora (2015). The impact of macroeconomic news on Polish and Czech government bond markets. https://openalex.org/W2280208800

114. Viacheslav M. Shavshukov, Natalia Zhuravleva (2020). Global Economy: New Risks and Leadership Problems. https://doi.org/10.3390/ijfs8010007

115. Christoph Boehm, T. Niklas Kroner (2024). Monetary Policy without Moving Interest Rates: The Fed Non-Yield Shock. https://doi.org/10.3386/w32636

116. Viacheslav M. Shavshukov, Natalia Zhuravleva (2020). Restructuring of the Global Economy. https://doi.org/10.20944/preprints202001.0235.v1

117. Vitaly Meursault, Pierre Jinghong Liang, Bryan Routledge et al. (2022). PEAD.txt: Post-Earnings-Announcement Drift Using Text. https://doi.org/10.1017/s0022109022001181

118. Herman Kamil, HKamil@imf.org (2008). Is Central Bank Intervention Effective Under Inflation Targeting Regimes? The Case of Colombia. https://doi.org/10.2139/ssrn.1119428

119. Peter Albrecht, Evžen Kočenda, Evžen Kočenda (2025). Event-driven changes in volatility connectedness in global forex markets. https://doi.org/10.1016/j.mulfin.2024.100896

120. Marko Hudak (2015). High Frequency Trading, International Markets, and Regulation. https://doi.org/10.1184/r1/6686054

121. Jiawei Wang, Zhe Chen (2024). Factor-GAN: Enhancing stock price prediction and factor investment with Generative Adversarial Networks. https://doi.org/10.1371/journal.pone.0306094

122. Ali Yeganeh, Sandile Charles Shongwe (2023). A novel application of statistical process control charts in financial market surveillance with the idea of profile monitoring. https://doi.org/10.1371/journal.pone.0288627

123. Markus Vogl (2022). Quantitative modelling frontiers: a literature review on the evolution in financial and risk modelling after the financial crisis (2008–2019). https://doi.org/10.1007/s43546-022-00359-3

124. Mesias Alfeus, Justin Harvey, Phuthehang Maphatsoe (2024). Improving realised volatility forecast for emerging markets. https://doi.org/10.1007/s12197-024-09701-x

125. Yuying Chen, Chiao-Ting Chen, Chuan-Yun Sang et al. (2021). Adversarial Attacks Against Reinforcement Learning-Based Portfolio Management Strategy. https://doi.org/10.1109/access.2021.3068768

126. Hanyao Gao, Gang Kou, Haiming Liang et al. (2024). Machine learning in business and finance: a literature review and research opportunities. https://doi.org/10.1186/s40854-024-00629-z

127. Carmen Reinhart, M. Belen Sbrancia (2011). The Liquidation of Government Debt. https://doi.org/10.1093/epolic/eiv003

128. Kristin J. Forbes, Francis E. Warnock (2011). Capital Flow Waves: Surges, Stops, Flight, and Retrenchment. https://doi.org/10.3386/w17351

129. Étienne Harb, Charbel Bassil, Talie Kassamany et al. (2022). Volatility Interdependence Between Cryptocurrencies, Equity, and Bond Markets. https://doi.org/10.1007/s10614-022-10318-7

130. Alexander Azerovich Musaev, Andrey Makshanov, D. Grigoriev (2022). Evolutionary Optimization of Control Strategies for Non-Stationary Immersion Environments. https://doi.org/10.3390/math10111797

131. Rohan Pothumsetty (2020). APPLICATION OF ARTIFICIAL INTELLIGENCE IN ALGORITHMIC TRADING. https://doi.org/10.33564/ijeast.2020.v04i12.019

132. Wipawan Buathong, Piroj Sieng-EK, Pita Jarupunphol (2023). Measuring the Performance of Machine Learning Forecasting Models to Support Bitcoin Investment Decisions. https://doi.org/10.47852/bonviewjdsis3202677

133. Sergiy Andriychuk (2025). CRYPTOCURRENCY VOLATILITY AND RISK MODELING: MONTE CARLO SIMULATIONS, GARCH ANALYSIS, AND FINANCIAL MARKET INTEGRATION. https://doi.org/10.36690/2674-5208-2025-1-98-115

134. Zezheng Zhang, Matloob Khushi (2020). GA-MSSR: Genetic Algorithm Maximizing Sharpe and Sterling Ratio Method for RoboTrading. https://doi.org/10.1109/ijcnn48605.2020.9206647

135. Ioannis Psaradellis, Jason Laws, Athanasios A. Pantelous et al. (2021). Technical analysis, spread trading, and data snooping control. https://doi.org/10.1016/j.ijforecast.2021.10.002

136. Shahzeb khan, Zawar Ahmed Khan, Saif Ur Rehman et al. (2025). Design and Implementation of a Multi-Strategy Algorithmic Trading Bot. https://doi.org/10.33411/ijist/20257315331541

137. Yu Gu (2012). Evaluating the effectiveness and sensitivity of forex trading robots. https://openalex.org/W2222909100

138. Jirásko Petr (2015). AOS - obchodní strategie založené na S/R úrovních technické analýzy. https://openalex.org/W2564858041

139. Ionuţ Nica, Ştefan Ionescu, Camelia Delcea et al. (2024). Quantitative Modeling of Financial Contagion: Unraveling Market Dynamics and Bubble Detection Mechanisms. https://doi.org/10.3390/risks12020036

140. Toby Daniel Watson (2009). On the profitability of technical trading. https://openalex.org/W1600005093

141. Tom C. W. Lin (2017). The New Market Manipulation. https://openalex.org/W2730618323

142. T. Soni Madhulatha, Md. Atheeq Sultan Ghori (2025). Deep neural network approach integrated with reinforcement learning for forecasting exchange rates using time series data and influential factors. https://doi.org/10.1038/s41598-025-12516-3

143. Lu Zhang, Lei Hua (2025). Major Issues in High-Frequency Financial Data Analysis: A Survey of Solutions. https://doi.org/10.3390/math13030347

144. Nikolaos Pippas, Elliot A. Ludvig, Çağatay Turkay (2024). The Evolution of Reinforcement Learning in Quantitative Finance: A Survey. https://doi.org/10.48550/arxiv.2408.10932

145. Paavani Jain, Ashok Ghimire (2025). Multi-factor forex hedging models: Merging geopolitical news and macroeconomic signals with reinforcement learning. https://doi.org/10.51594/estj.v6i3.1881

146. Kari Kostiainen (2016). Development of Trading Algorithm Backtest Environment. https://openalex.org/W2341875285

147. Riris Shanti, Hermanto Siregar, Nimmi Zulbainarni et al. (2023). Role of Digital Transformation on Digital Business Model Banks. https://doi.org/10.3390/su152316293

148. Darko Vuković, Michael Frömmel, Samuel A. Vigne et al. (2024). Spillovers between cryptocurrencies and financial markets in a global framework. https://doi.org/10.1016/j.jimonfin.2024.103235

149. Li-Chen Cheng, Wei-Ting Lu, Benjamin Yeo (2023). Predicting abnormal trading behavior from internet rumor propagation: a machine learning approach. https://doi.org/10.1186/s40854-022-00423-9

150. Ikhlaas Gurrib, Firuz Kamalov, Olga Starkova et al. (2023). Performance of Equity Investments in Sustainable Environmental Markets. https://doi.org/10.3390/su15097453

151. Marco Rocco (2012). Extreme Value Theory for Finance: A Survey. https://doi.org/10.2139/ssrn.1998740

152. Carol L. Osler (2002). Stop-loss orders and price cascades in currency markets. https://openalex.org/W3125804786

153. Adrian Millea, Abbas Edalat (2022). Using Deep Reinforcement Learning with Hierarchical Risk Parity for Portfolio Optimization. https://doi.org/10.3390/ijfs11010010

154. Mehmet Sahiner (2023). Volatility Spillovers and Contagion During Major Crises: An Early Warning Approach Based on a Deep Learning Model. https://doi.org/10.1007/s10614-023-10412-4

155. Takumi Sueshige, Didier Sornette, Hideki Takayasu et al. (2019). Classification of position management strategies at the order-book level and their influences on future market-price formation. https://doi.org/10.1371/journal.pone.0220645

156. Ila Patnaik (2003). India's policy stance on reserves and the currency. https://openalex.org/W1548487022

157. Pejman Peykani, Mostafa Sargolzaei, Mohammad Hashem Botshekan et al. (2023). Optimization of Asset and Liability Management of Banks with Minimum Possible Changes. https://doi.org/10.3390/math11122761

158. Timo Klein (2020). Essays in competition economics. https://openalex.org/W3093039303

159. Jean-Philippe Bouchaud, J. Doyne Farmer, Fabrizio Lillo (2008). How markets slowly digest changes in supply and demand. https://doi.org/10.48550/arxiv.0809.0822

160. Soham Pathak, Antara Pawar, Shruti Taware et al. (2023). A Survey on Machine Learning Algorithms for Risk-Controlled Algorithmic Trading. https://doi.org/10.32628/ijsrst523103163

161. Raj Gaurav Mishra, Dharmendra Sharma, Mahipal Yasuman Gadhavi et al. (2025). A Deep Reinforcement Learning Framework for

Strategic Indian NIFTY 50 Index Trading. https://doi.org/10.3390/ai6080183

162. Nabeel Ahmad Saidd (2026). Decomposable Reward Modeling and Realistic Environment Design for Reinforcement Learning-Based Forex Trading. https://doi.org/10.20944/preprints202603.1701.v1

163. Deniz Noormohammadzadehmaleki, Mahdi Mirzabaki (2025). FMARL: A Novel Hybrid Model Finite Machine Automata and Deep Reinforcement Learning Algorithm for Futures Market Forecasting and Trading System. https://doi.org/10.36227/techrxiv.175987727.73143592/v1

164. Aleš Zamuda, Vincenzo Crescimanna, Juan C. Burguillo et al. (2019). Forecasting Cryptocurrency Value by Sentiment Analysis: An HPC-Oriented Survey of the State-of-the-Art in the Cloud Era. https://doi.org/10.1007/978-3-030-16272-6_12

165. Satyam Kumar, Yelleti Vivek, Vadlamani Ravi et al. (2023). Causal Inference for Banking Finance and Insurance A Survey. https://doi.org/10.48550/arxiv.2307.16427

166. Ali Rahmad, Fatchur Rozi, Andy Rachman et al. (2025). PROTOTYPING MODEL FOR DESIGNING A DESKTOP-BASED TRADING ROBOT APPLICATION. https://doi.org/10.56943/joe.v4i4.882

167. sirous keshavarz, Parisa Alizadeh, Zahra Mostafaie et al. (2025). Modeling the Impact of Aggressive Financial Behavior on Financial Decision-Making: Evidence from Forex Market Investors. https://doi.org/10.21203/rs.3.rs-6519925/v1

168. Stanislav Parfenov (2025). Psychological Factors and Their Effects on Investment Decision-Making Among Private Investors in the Modern Financial Era : Theory and Evidence from Behavioral Finance with Case Analysis. https://openalex.org/W7116815521

169. Michael J. Randall (2019). Adoption of a financial transaction tax in Europe through flexible integration. https://openalex.org/W2944070696

170. Unknown author (2024). Materials of the XXIV Annual International Conference. https://doi.org/10.36994/978-966-388-714-2-2024-2

171. Petro Talanchuk (2024). INCLUSIVE EDUCATIONAL ENVIRONMENT: PROBLEMS, PROSPECTS, BEST PRACTICES. https://doi.org/10.36994/978-966-388-714-2-2024-2-584

172. Ч. Гу (2025). Исследование факторов влияния и потенциала развития трансграничной электронной торговли между Китаем и Россией.. https://openalex.org/W7140066054

173. Karyn Munyengeterwa (2020). Financial inclusion technologies and bank performance: insights from Zimbabwe's banking sector. https://openalex.org/W3130073923

174. Qin Wang, Guangsheng Yu, Shiping Chen (2023). Cryptocurrency in the Aftermath: Unveiling the Impact of the SVB Collapse. https://doi.org/10.36227/techrxiv.24247855.v1

175. International Science Group, Denis Vladlenov (2025). TECHNOLOGIES FOR IMPROVING OLD METHODS, THEORIES AND HYPOTHESES. https://doi.org/10.46299/isg.p.2025.1.1

176. Qin Wang, Guangsheng Yu, Shiping Chen (2023). Cryptocurrency in the Aftermath: Unveiling the Impact of the SVB Collapse. https://doi.org/10.36227/techrxiv.24247855

177. Qin Wang, Guangsheng Yu, Shiping Chen (2023). Cryptocurrency in the Aftermath: Unveiling the Impact of the SVB Collapse. https://doi.org/10.48550/arxiv.2311.10720

178. Viral V. Acharya, Soumya Bhadury, Jay Surti (2020). Financial Vulnerability and Risks to Growth in Emerging Markets. https://doi.org/10.3386/w27411

179. Shiye He (2015). Topological optimisation of artificial neural networks for financial asset forecasting. https://openalex.org/W2297367780

180. Sibaram Prasad Panda (2025). Artificial Intelligence Across Borders: Transforming Industries Through Intelligent Innovation. https://doi.org/10.70593/978-93-49910-25-6

181. Tomasz Witkowski, Tomasz Wachowicz, Krzysztof Kania (2025). Self-augmenting Technical Indicator with Recurrent Reinforcement Learning. https://doi.org/10.21203/rs.3.rs-7312949/v1

182. Amparo Soler-Dominguez, Ángel A. Juan, Renatas Kizys (2017). A Survey on Financial Applications of Metaheuristics. https://doi.org/10.1145/3054133

183. Srinivasa Rao Challa (2025). Real-time financial decision systems for trading, investment planning, and risk management. https://doi.org/10.70593/978-93-49910-98-0_10

184. SONIA KHOSA (2025). Deeper, Strategic Collaboration in the Securities Sector. https://doi.org/10.2307/jj.38479247

185. Zhaoyang Zhao (2008). Chemometrics-derived methods and statistical techniques to model and forecast futures markets. https://doi.org/10.17760/d10016752

186. Ziwei Yi, Xinwei Cao, Zuyan Chen et al. (2023). Artificial Intelligence in Accounting and Finance: Challenges and Opportunities. https://doi.org/10.1109/access.2023.3333389

187. Andrew Huang, Matloob Khushi, Basem Suleiman (2023). Regime-Specific Quant Generative Adversarial Network: A Conditional Generative Adversarial Network for Regime-Specific Deepfakes of Financial Time Series. https://doi.org/10.3390/app131910639

188. Joseph Zhi Bin Ling, Albert K. Tsui, Zhaoyong Zhang (2021). Trading Macro-Cycles of Foreign Exchange Markets Using Hybrid Models. https://doi.org/10.3390/su13179820

189. Steven L. Schwarcz (2021). Regulating Global Stablecoins: A Model-Law Strategy. https://doi.org/10.2139/ssrn.3966569

190. Daniel Vincent Oberholtzer (2011). Margin-at-Risk for Agricultural Processors: Flour Milling Scenarios. https://openalex.org/W2950423995

Conclusion

What separates a durable forex trader from a short-lived one is not the ability to find the occasional strong setup. It is the ability to keep making sound decisions when conditions are uneven, when the market is quiet, when volatility expands without warning, and when a trade sequence does not unfold the way you expected. That standard is higher than simply being “right” on a chart. It requires a process that can absorb uncertainty without losing structure.

By this point, the important pieces should fit together as one workflow. The market context tells you what kind of environment you are in. Price action and technical tools help you identify whether a setup has structure. Fundamental conditions explain why a currency pair may be under pressure or gaining support. Risk management determines whether a valid idea is worth taking and how much capital belongs on the line. Trade execution and order management turn the plan into an actual position. Psychology and routine keep the entire process from breaking down under pressure.

If any one of those pieces is missing, the weakness usually shows up somewhere else. A trader may have a good entry model but no meaningful stop structure. Another may understand macro drivers but still size positions too aggressively. Another may journal every trade but fail to act on the patterns the journal reveals. The point is not to become perfect in every area. The point is to make each part of the process strong enough that it supports the others.

That also means accepting that improvement in forex is rarely dramatic. It is usually incremental. A better stop placement here, a cleaner entry there, one avoided revenge trade, one week of proper review, one reduction in oversized risk. Those small changes matter because trading results are cumulative. Over time, the difference between a trader who respects the process and one who improvises becomes visible in drawdowns, consistency, and emotional stability.

The market will continue to change. Session behavior shifts, volatility expands and contracts, central bank expectations evolve, and correlations can break down when conditions change. A strategy that works well in one phase may struggle in another. That is not a reason to abandon structure; it is a reason to keep evaluating whether the structure still fits the environment. A trader who treats the market as fixed will eventually be surprised. A trader who treats the market as adaptive can respond without panic.

This is where discipline becomes practical rather than abstract. Discipline is not simply resisting temptation. It is making your trading rules easier to follow than your impulses. It is defining risk before entry, checking whether the setup still meets your criteria, stepping away when there is no edge, and reviewing your performance without self-deception. The more consistent those habits become, the less trading depends on mood.

It is also worth remembering that sustainability matters more than intensity. A trader who pushes too hard, takes too many marginal trades, or stays mentally engaged long after focus has faded is usually not building an advantage. They are wearing down the very judgment they need. Long-term progress comes from preserving decision quality. That means protecting energy, respecting your limits, and recognizing that rest is part of performance, not a break from it.

The tools in this book are meant to work together in that spirit. None of them is powerful enough on its own to guarantee success, but together they create a framework for trading with more clarity and less guesswork. When you know what market conditions you are trading, what setup you are waiting for, how much you are willing to lose, and how you will review the result, you are no longer reacting blindly. You are operating with a method.

That method will still be tested. You will have losing trades, periods of uncertainty, and moments when your confidence or patience is strained. Those moments are not proof that the process has failed. They are part of the process. What matters is whether you continue to apply the same standards when the market becomes inconvenient.

A trader who can do that has something valuable: not certainty, but control over the parts that can actually be controlled. In forex, that is the foundation of survival, and survival is what gives skill enough time to turn into consistency.

Appendix: Practical Forex Tools and Reference Materials

The material that follows is designed to make the trading process easier to apply when you are away from the main discussion and need a working reference. Instead of revisiting the theory behind entries, exits, and market behavior, this appendix gathers a few practical tools that support consistent execution and review. The templates and reference points here are meant to be used, adapted, and kept close at hand as part of an active routine, not read once and set aside. As with the rest of the book, the emphasis is on structure: clear decisions, controlled risk, and a repeatable process that can be checked against your own results.

Sample trading plan template and pre-trade checklist

A trading plan template works best when it is specific enough to remove guesswork but simple enough to use consistently. The purpose is not to create a document that looks impressive; it is to define the exact conditions under which you will trade, how much you will risk, and what you will do once the trade is live. A useful template should fit on one or two pages and be written in plain language. If you cannot explain a rule clearly on paper, it is usually too vague to guide real decisions in a fast-moving market.

A practical template begins with the basics of identity and scope: the pairs you trade, the time frames you use, and the style you follow. Then it moves into the decision rules. For example, a trader may define the trend filter, the setup conditions, the trigger for entry, the stop-loss location, the initial profit target, and the maximum risk per trade. It should also state what conditions disqualify a trade, such as a major news release, unusually wide spreads, or a setup that appears valid on one time frame but conflicts with a higher-time-frame structure. Research on trading system development consistently shows that rule clarity and repeatability matter more than subjective judgment when evaluating performance over time [3][67].

A written plan should also include personal constraints. These are the limits that protect you from drifting into overtrading or oversized exposure when the market becomes exciting. That may include a maximum number of trades per day, a daily loss limit, a weekly drawdown limit, and a rule for stopping after a sequence of losses. If you trade multiple pairs, the plan should address whether correlated positions count as one risk idea or several. This matters because the market can expose you to the same currency theme through different instruments at once, even when the charts look separate. The goal is to make your risk boundaries explicit before emotions or urgency can blur them.

A simple template can be organized around a few fixed prompts:

- Market focus: Which pairs and sessions are allowed?
- Setup criteria: What must be present before a trade is considered?
- Entry trigger: What exact event confirms the entry?
- Stop-loss rule: Where is the trade invalidated?
- Target or exit rule: How is profit taken or the trade closed?
- Risk limits: How much is risked per trade, per day, and per week?
- No-trade conditions: When should you stand aside?
- Review rule: What must be recorded after the trade?

That structure keeps the plan from becoming a vague statement of intent. It turns it into a decision tool.

The pre-trade checklist should be even more operational. It is the final filter used immediately before placing an order, when it is easy to skip steps because the setup looks attractive. A good checklist forces the trader to verify both the market and the trade itself. First, confirm that the broader context still supports the idea. Then confirm that the entry is aligned with the plan, that the stop-loss is placed at a logical invalidation point, and that the position size matches the account risk rule. Only after those items are checked should the order be placed. In many cases, the best use of a checklist is not to help you take more trades, but to help you reject the wrong ones.

A disciplined pre-trade checklist might include the following questions:

1. Is this pair on my approved watchlist?
2. Does the current session fit my strategy?
3. Is the higher-time-frame context supportive?
4. Has a valid setup formed according to my rules?
5. Is there a clear trigger for entry?
6. Is the stop-loss placed where the setup is invalidated?
7. Does the position size keep risk within my limit?
8. Is the risk-to-reward ratio acceptable?
9. Are spreads, news, or volatility conditions acceptable?
10. Have I written down the reason for the trade?

The final item is often overlooked, but it is one of the most useful. Writing down the reason for the trade before entry creates accountability and improves later review. If the trade is taken for a reason that cannot be stated clearly, it is usually not a trade that belongs in the plan. That simple habit also makes journaling more accurate, because you are recording the decision while it is still honest rather than reconstructing it after the outcome is known.

The most effective traders treat the plan and checklist as living documents. They are stable enough to enforce discipline, but not so rigid that they ignore evidence from actual performance. If a rule repeatedly protects you from bad trades, keep it. If a rule is too broad, too narrow, or impossible to follow in real time, revise it after review rather than in the middle of a position. The point is to create a process that can be used under pressure without improvisation. A plan that is clear on paper and a checklist that is used before every order do more than organize trades; they reduce avoidable errors and make your results easier to study, which is where sustainable improvement begins.

Risk management worksheet and position sizing reference

A risk management worksheet turns abstract rules into numbers you can act on before a trade is placed. It should answer, in plain terms, how much equity is in the account, how much can be risked on the next trade, where the stop belongs, what that stop means in dollar terms, and what position size keeps the loss inside the limit. If those numbers are not written down, traders tend to improvise when a setup appears, and improvisation is where risk drift begins. The worksheet is not meant to predict outcomes; it is meant to make the cost of being wrong known in advance.

A practical worksheet can be built around a few fields that are filled out every time. Start with account equity, then define the maximum percentage risk per trade, the stop distance in pips or price units, the pair being traded, and the planned entry price. From there, the worksheet should convert the stop distance into monetary risk and then into lot size. A simple structure might look like this:

- Account equity: the current account balance or equity before entry
- Risk per trade: the fixed percentage or dollar amount you are willing to lose
- Entry price: the price at which the trade will be opened
- Stop-loss price: the price level where the setup is invalidated
- Stop distance: the gap between entry and stop, measured in pips or points
- Position size: the number of units, mini lots, or standard lots that keeps the loss within the limit
- Target price: the planned exit if the trade reaches the intended reward area
- Risk-to-reward ratio: the projected reward compared with the defined risk

The key is to treat the worksheet as a decision filter, not a record you complete after the fact. If the setup requires a stop so wide that the position size becomes too small to justify the trade, that is useful information. If the stop is so tight that normal price noise is likely to hit it before the idea has room to work, that is also useful information. In both cases, the worksheet helps you judge whether the trade belongs in your plan at all. Many losses are not caused by bad direction; they are caused by entering with a structure that does not fit the account.

Position sizing reference is the companion to the worksheet because it translates risk into trade size across different account types. The general formula is straightforward: position size = amount at risk ÷ stop value per unit. The exact stop value depends on the pair, the quote currency, and the broker's contract specifications, but the principle remains the same. A trader risking $100 on a trade with a 25-pip stop should size the position so that a full stop-out costs about $100, not $150 or $250. That discipline matters because leverage can magnify the difference between a controlled loss and a damaging one. The market does not care whether the account is large or small; the sizing method has to keep the exposure proportional to the account.

For many traders, it helps to use a fixed-risk framework rather than adjusting risk based on confidence. For example, a trader might decide that every standard setup risks 0.5% of equity, while only the highest-quality setups are allowed 1%. The point is consistency. If account equity is $10,000 and the chosen risk is 1%, the maximum planned loss is $100. If the stop on EUR/USD is 20 pips, the position size must be calculated so that 20 pips equals roughly $100. If the stop is 50 pips, the position size must be reduced accordingly. This keeps the trade aligned with the plan even when the chart conditions change from one pair to another.

A good reference sheet should also remind you that not all risk is visible in the stop-loss. Spread, slippage, and correlated exposure can make the real risk larger than the chart suggests. If a trade is placed around a news event or in a fast-moving session, the expected loss at the stop may not be the actual loss. If you are already holding positions in pairs that share the same base currency or respond to the same macro theme, the new trade may increase portfolio risk more than the worksheet implies. For that reason, the reference should include a line for open exposure so you can see whether the account is already carrying too much directional risk.

It is also useful to keep a quick conversion guide near the worksheet so you are not recalculating basic values under pressure. A trader can note the pip value for the most frequently traded pair sizes, the maximum number of simultaneous trades allowed, and the preferred minimum risk-to-reward ratio for valid setups. Over time, this creates a habit of making decisions the same way every time: define the setup, define the invalidation point, calculate the size, and then decide whether the trade still deserves capital. That sequence protects the account from emotional sizing, which is one of the fastest ways to turn a decent method into uneven results.

The worksheet works best when it is simple enough to use before every order. If it takes too long, traders stop using it; if it is too vague, it stops protecting the account. The most effective version is usually one page, filled in the same order each time, with enough structure to remove guesswork and enough flexibility to handle different pairs and time frames. The goal is not to make trading slower for its own sake. The goal is to make sure every position begins with a defined loss, a defined size, and a defined purpose.

Glossary of essential forex terms and concepts

Forex trading has its own vocabulary, and that vocabulary matters because small differences in meaning can lead to large differences in execution. A trader who understands the terms clearly is better equipped to read a chart, interpret a broker's pricing, and follow a plan without confusion. The goal here is not to memorize jargon for its own sake, but to build a working language that supports consistent decision-making.

A currency pair is the basic quote format in forex. The first currency is the base currency, and the second is the quote currency. If EUR/USD is trading at 1.0850, that means one euro is worth 1.0850 U.S. dollars. When the pair rises, the base currency is strengthening relative to the quote currency; when it falls, the base currency is weakening. This structure is important because every trade in forex is a relative value decision, not a simple "up or down" bet on one currency alone.

Pips, pipettes, and lot size are among the most practical terms in the market. A pip is the standard unit used to measure price movement in most currency pairs, while a pipette is a fractional pip, often used to show finer price increments. Lot size describes the number of units traded. A standard lot is larger than a mini lot or micro lot, and the size you choose directly affects how much money you gain or lose for each pip of movement. That is why a trader can have a good setup and still take on excessive risk simply by trading too large. The chart may look the same, but the account impact will not.

Spread, commission, and slippage all affect the real cost of trading. The spread is the difference between the bid and ask price, and it is one of the ways brokers are compensated. Commission is a separate fee charged on some account types. Slippage occurs when the price you receive is different from the price you expected, usually because the market moved quickly or liquidity was thin. These costs matter most when a strategy depends on frequent entries, tight stops, or short holding periods. A setup that appears profitable before costs can become much less attractive once execution expenses are included.

Liquidity refers to how easily a market can absorb buying and selling without large price disruption. In highly liquid pairs, orders are usually filled more smoothly and spreads tend to be tighter. In less liquid pairs, price can jump more sharply, spreads may widen, and execution can become less predictable. Related to liquidity is volatility, which describes the degree of price movement over a given period. A market can be liquid but still volatile, especially during major news events. Traders should not confuse the two: liquidity affects how easily trades are executed, while volatility affects how far and how fast price may move.

Leverage and margin are closely linked and must be understood before any real capital is put at risk. Leverage allows a trader to control a larger position with a smaller amount of capital, which can magnify both gains and losses. Margin is the portion of account equity set aside to support that leveraged position. Because leverage can make small market moves feel large, it is one of the main reasons risk management must be defined before entry. A trader who uses leverage without discipline is not trading more efficiently; they are simply increasing the speed at which mistakes can damage the account.

Stop-loss, take-profit, and risk-to-reward ratio are terms that define how a trade is managed before it is placed. A stop-loss is the predetermined exit point where the trade idea is considered invalid. A take-profit is the level where gains will be realized if the market moves as expected. The risk-to-reward ratio compares the amount being risked to the amount being targeted. For example, risking 20 pips to seek 40 pips creates a 1:2 ratio. That ratio does not guarantee success, but it helps a trader evaluate whether the potential reward justifies the risk being taken.

A few more terms appear constantly in chart analysis and order management. A breakout occurs when price moves beyond a well-defined level, such as support or resistance. A pullback is a temporary retracement against the prevailing move. A trend is the broader directional tendency of price, while range or consolidation describes a market moving sideways between boundaries. Support is a zone where buying has previously emerged, and resistance is a zone where selling has previously appeared. These are not fixed walls, but areas where behavior has changed before and may do so again.

Finally, it helps to distinguish between market order, limit order, and stop order. A market order seeks immediate execution at the best available price. A limit order seeks a specific price or better. A stop order becomes active once price reaches a trigger level and is often used to enter with momentum or to protect an existing position. In practice, these order types are tools for translating a trading plan into action. The more clearly you understand them, the less likely you are to improvise under pressure.

Some terms do not describe price mechanics directly, but they shape the trader's environment. A broker is the intermediary through which trades are placed. A demo account allows practice without real capital, while a live account exposes the trader to actual financial risk. A drawdown is the decline from a peak in account equity, and it is one of the clearest measures of how well risk is being controlled. A trader who can read these terms accurately is better positioned to judge both opportunity and exposure with the discipline the market demands.

Suggested routine for continued study and practice

A useful study routine is not built around motivation; it is built around repetition that keeps your analysis sharp and your execution honest. The goal is to stay in contact with the market often enough that patterns remain familiar, but not so often that you start confusing activity with progress. For most traders, that means working from a short list of pairs that match the style you trade, reviewing them at the same time each day, and using the same sequence of checks every time. Consistency matters because your edge is easier to evaluate when your process is stable. If the routine changes from day to day, it becomes difficult to tell whether your results came from skill, luck, or a different way of looking at the chart.

Begin each study session by reviewing what the market has already done, not by hunting for a trade immediately. Check the higher time frame first so you can see whether the pair is trending, ranging, compressing, or reacting to a major level. Then move to the execution time frame and ask whether the lower-time-frame behavior is aligned with the larger structure. This habit keeps you from taking isolated signals that look attractive on a smaller chart but are poorly aligned with the broader context. It also trains you to think in terms of market conditions, which is more durable than memorizing a single setup. The more clearly you can define the environment, the easier it becomes to know which strategy deserves attention and which one should be left alone.

After the chart review, spend time on deliberate practice rather than passive observation. One effective method is to mark past setups and replay them bar by bar, forcing yourself to make the same decisions you would make in real time. Note where the setup became valid, where it failed, and whether your planned stop, target, and position size would have been appropriate. This kind of review is especially valuable because it exposes the difference between recognizing a setup in hindsight and executing it under uncertainty. It also helps you refine your rules without risking capital while you are still learning how your strategy behaves across different market conditions. Over time, you should be able to explain not only what worked, but why it worked and when it was likely to fail.

Keep a written record of your study sessions in the same way you keep a trading journal. Record the pair, date, time frame, setup type, market condition, and the specific lesson you learned. If a trade was missed, write down whether the miss came from hesitation, poor preparation, or a valid decision to stay out. If a trade was taken, document whether it followed the plan and whether the result came from execution quality or from the market simply moving in your favor. This record turns vague impressions into usable data. Without it, traders often repeat the same mistakes because memory tends to preserve outcomes more vividly than process. With it, you begin to see patterns in your own behavior, which is often more important than the pattern on the chart.

A weekly review should be more than a glance at wins and losses. Set aside time to evaluate whether your trades came from the conditions your strategy was designed to handle. If you trade breakouts, were you taking them in periods of compression and expansion, or were you forcing them in low-energy conditions? If you trade ranges, were you respecting the boundaries, or were you trying to fade every minor fluctuation? This is also the right time to review risk consistency. A strategy can appear profitable while still being undermined by oversized positions, poor stop placement, or inconsistent execution. The purpose of the review is to identify whether your process is repeatable, not just whether the last few trades were profitable.

To keep your practice effective, limit the number of things you are trying to improve at once. A trader who changes entry logic, risk size, chart layout, and time frame all in the same week will not know which adjustment caused the result. Choose one skill to focus on for a defined period, such as waiting for cleaner confirmations, placing stops more logically, or reducing impulsive entries. That narrower focus makes improvement easier to measure and prevents the routine from becoming overwhelming. It also fits the reality of market learning: skill develops through small, repeated corrections, not through constant reinvention. As algorithmic and technology-driven trading have expanded across financial markets, the value of disciplined process has only increased, because traders are competing in an environment where speed, structure, and consistency matter more than ever [32].

Make room in the routine for non-chart study as well. Read about the economic themes, policy shifts, and market structure issues that influence the pairs you trade. You do not need to become a macroeconomist to trade well, but you do need enough context to understand why a pair may behave differently from one week to the next. A routine that includes both chart work and background study builds better judgment than one that relies only on pattern recognition. Over time, the objective is to develop a process that keeps you learning without overloading you. If you can return to the same routine day after day, review your decisions honestly, and make small improvements with discipline, your study time becomes part of your trading edge rather than a separate activity.

www.ingramcontent.com/pod-product-compliance
Lightning Source LLC
LaVergne TN
LVHW100315210926
848480LV00003B/1132
* 9 7 8 1 9 2 3 8 1 7 7 6 0 *